RENEWALS 458-4574

DATE DUE

GAYLORD			PRINTED IN U.S.A.

UNDERSTANDING PSYCHOTHERAPY CHANGE

UNDERSTANDING PSYCHOTHERAPY CHANGE

A PRACTICAL GUIDE TO CONFIGURATIONAL ANALYSIS

MARDI HOROWITZ

American Psychological Association • Washington, DC

Published by
American Psychological Association
750 First Street, NE
Washington, DC 20002
www.apa.org

To order
APA Order Department
P.O. Box 92984
Washington, DC 20090-2984
Tel: (800) 374-2721
Direct: (202) 336-5510
Fax: (202) 336-5502
TDD/TTY: (202) 336-6123
Online: www.apa.org/books/
E-mail: order@apa.org

In the U.K., Europe, Africa, and the Middle East, copies may be ordered from
American Psychological Association
3 Henrietta Street
Covent Garden, London
WC2E 8LU England

Typeset in Goudy by World Composition Services, Inc., Sterling, VA

Printer: Victor Graphics, Inc., Baltimore, MD
Cover Designer: Naylor Design, Washington, DC
Project Manager: Debbie Hardin, Carlsbad, CA

The opinions and statements published are the responsibility of the author, and such opinions and statements do not necessarily represent the policies of the American Psychological Association.

Library of Congress Cataloging-in-Publication Data

Horowitz, Mardi Jon, 1934–
    Understanding psychotherapy change : a practical guide to configurational analysis / Mardi Horowitz.
        p. cm.
    Includes bibliographical references and index.
    ISBN 1-59147-228-8
    1. Psychotherapy—Methodology. I. Title.

    RC480.5.H673   2005
    616.89'14—dc22   2004021053

British Library Cataloguing-in-Publication Data
A CIP record is available from the British Library.

Printed in the United States of America
First edition

For my grandchildren (so far),
Wesley, Paloma, Jack, Elijah, Leilani, Ari, and Lahela.

CONTENTS

Foreword .... *ix*

Preface .... *xi*

Introduction 3

I. Case Formulation **15**

Chapter 1.   Janice's Case and Steps 1 Through 4 17

Chapter 2.   Steps 1 and 2: Describing Phenomena and
              States of Mind 27

Chapter 3.   Step 3: Formulating Topics of Concern
              and Defensive Control Processes 47

Chapter 4.   Step 4: Exploring Identity and Relationships 55

II. Mid-Course Corrections **69**

Chapter 5.   Steps 5 and 6: Modifying States and State
              Transitions and Working Through Topics
              of Concern 71

Chapter 6.   Step 7: Working on Views of Self
              and Relationships 87

III. Evaluation and Treatment Outcome **99**

Chapter 7.   Step 8: Evaluating Change 101

Chapter 8.   Review of Configurational Analysis 113

Epilogue 119

Glossary 121

References 125

Index 133

About the Author 139

FOREWORD

JEROME L. SINGER

In the mid-1930s, a young American psychologist, Saul Rosenzweig (deceased in 2004 at age 97), wrote to Sigmund Freud to describe his experimental research with normal individuals, studies that lent some support to the theory of repression. Freud wrote back to Rosenzweig thanking him for his interest but pointing out that laboratory research could not really contribute to the theory that was best derived from the clinical psychoanalytical process. Somewhat condescendingly, Freud added, "But there is little harm in your effort."

About 20 years later when I was one of the early psychologist candidates admitted to a psychoanalytical institute, a famous analyst, Erich Fromm, dismissed my comments about the necessity for research studying how emotions interacted with basic cognitive processes in generating motivation by calling such work "mere academic psychology."

Mardi Horowitz, from his earliest days in psychiatry, has been committed to integrating psychotherapy and psychoanalytical theory with the data and constructs of fundamental behavioral science research on cognitive and affective processes. His continuing interest has been in the conscious stream of thought and its relationship to the unconscious mental processes that seem to be illuminated by the clinical data of psychoanalysis. We first met about 40 years ago when, as a young psychiatrist starting a research as well as a clinical career, he visited the laboratory on consciousness and cognition that John Antrobus and I had established at the City College of New York. Horowitz had begun a series of important experimental studies on the contingent circumstances that led particular stressful or traumatic experiences to generate intrusive or peremptory ideation patterns into the flow of normal thought. He also pioneered the study of other constituents of thought, especially visual imagery, which he showed to be especially relevant to the psychotherapeutic process. The fine work he did integrating laboratory research and clinical service undoubtedly accounted for his selection by the MacArthur Foundation to direct their national research program on conscious and unconscious mental processes. In the course of this decade of combined laboratory and clinical studies he brought together for consultation, theory construction, and collaborative research some of the most gifted cognitive scientists and psychodynamically oriented experimenters.

In many ways this volume reflects the influence of the rich research outcomes of this impressive effort, winnowed through the particular combination of clinical sensitivity and broad scholarship that is Horowitz's special gift. He has directed his effort in this book to examining how the linkages between moods or states of mind, cognitive processing, motivations, and the therapeutic alliance of client and practitioner can identify adaptive and maladaptive role relationships and lead to effective change in personalities. In these days when psychology and psychiatry may have veered too sharply (perhaps under insurance company pressures) in the direction of a narrow, traditional medical-model, symptom-reduction focus, he has drawn on research evidence and clinical experience to support a more person-centered and surely effective psychotherapeutic orientation. One finds in this volume implications derived from cognitive science's research on schemas and scripts as critical features of mental organization, from studies of self-schemas and the discrepancies between actual and ideal self-descriptions conducted in social psychology as well as from Horowitz and collaborators' own studies of conscious and unconscious mental processes as they emerge in therapeutic interactions. This solid underpinning of basic research is directed toward the practical concerns and efforts of the committed clinician. In addition to its solid basis in broad-ranging technical research, the material on producing clinical change is presented in a clear and direct fashion. After a half century of effort myself as a clinician and psychological scientist, I strongly urge readers, whether practitioners or researchers, to study this book with care and to apply what they can to an integrative scientist–practitioner effort in the best tradition of mental and behavioral science.

PREFACE

In this book, I present a systematic way to formulate the answers to the following questions: What changes in psychotherapy are desirable? How does change come about? What *does* change? The method is called configurational analysis. I developed configurational analysis by integrating different schools of thought about what happens in symptom formation and psychotherapy, taking the perspectives of both cognitive science and psychodynamics. The result of these efforts was a book called *States of Mind* (Horowitz, 1979, 1987).

Each component of configurational analysis was revised and upgraded through clinical research efforts that followed the publication of *States of Mind*. These investigative methods were summarized in *Person Schemas and Maladaptive Interpersonal Patterns* (Horowitz, 1991b). The emergent theory was highlighted in *Cognitive Psychodynamics: From Conflict to Character* (Horowitz, 1998). Configurational analysis was presented as a pragmatic approach to initial case evaluation in *Formulation as a Basis for Planning Psychotherapy Treatment* (Horowitz, 1997, 2002a). Since 1997, I have amplified the system, resulting in the work presented in this book.

I developed this material through years of teaching psychotherapy beginners, so it is written at a level suitable for trainees. Although the system has dynamic depth, allowing for inferences about not-so-conscious motives, it is most sharply focused on what can be observed, including defensive states. The system allows for understanding often complex emotional issues, and it can be used as a basis for planning any kind of technique or technical combinations. By learning this sytem trainees will acquire new abilities to discern the subtle variations in the state of another person, as well as themselves in the context of doing therapy. I also hope that some readers will go on to study how change occurs, in different types of conditions, different types of individuals, and with new integrations of psychotherapy techniques, which would advance our field in a much needed direction.

The goal of my clinical research has been to work with others in the field to develop an integrated theory as a basis for psychotherapy. In doing so I was fortunate to have the financial support of the University of California, San Francisco; the National Institute of Mental Health; and the John D. and Catherine T. MacArthur Foundation. Theory time was well supported by two separated years at the Center for Advanced Study in Behavioral Sciences at Stanford University. My main collaborators included George Bonanno, Paul Crits-Cristoph, Katherine DeWitt, Tracy Eells, Robert Emde, Matthew Erdelyi, Mary Ewert, Jess Ghannam, Dianna Hartley, Michael Hoyt, Nancy Kaltreider, Janice Krupnick, Lester Luborsky, Henry Markman, Charles Marmar, Thomas Merluzzi, Aubrey Metcalf, Constance Milbrath, Robert Rosenbaum, Peter Salovey, Jerome Singer, Alan Skolnikoff, Charles Stinson, Eva Sundin, Sandra Tunis, Robert Wallerstein, Nancy Wilner, and Hans Znoj.

I am grateful to my patient Janice (not her true name), whose consent to use her therapy for research and teaching purposes was invaluable. Carol Horowitz, Linda McCarter, Damien Moskowitz, Margarite Salinas, Malique Carr, and Debbie Hardin read drafts of the manuscript and worked hard to put this book together.

Earlier I mentioned theoretical integration. That refers to psychology's need as a discipline to put together a general approach to psychotherapy. We should not dissociate but rather we should combine cognitive, behavioral, interpersonal, supportive, and psychodynamic psychotherapies. The states of mind and person-schemas language used in this beginners' textbook permits such an integration.

UNDERSTANDING PSYCHOTHERAPY CHANGE

INTRODUCTION

A clinician begins with a provisional case formulation and initial plan for how to proceed with treatment. As the therapy progresses, the clinician augments this formulation and changes plans for intervention accordingly. The clinician may share some aspects of the formulation with the patient, who is also engaged in his or her own self-formulation. When some parts of the patient's own formulation do not accord with the therapist's case formulation, the therapist may suggest that they compare views. However, this sharing is not indicated in all cases.

As therapy proceeds, the clinician analyzes the processes of change and revises initial formulations, making appropriate mid-course corrections to his or her interventions. The clinician also formulates the intended outcome of treatment from the first session to the last. So, as therapy proceeds, the clinician can use a systematic approach anytime during the treatment to (a) update the initial case formulation, (b) examine how and why change is occurring, and (c) consider outcome thus far.

At the close of therapy and during periods of time after termination, the clinician also arranges for additional evaluation of treatment outcome. However, practicalities of therapy conducted in nonresearch settings often render this step ideal rather than actual.

This book presents a systematic method of case formulation, intervention, and evaluation of outcome. The book is intended for advanced graduate students in psychology, psychiatry, and social work, for novice postgraduate psychotherapists, and for experienced psychotherapists adjusting to a managed care environment that emphasizes clear formulation.

The case formulation, intervention, and evaluation presented in this volume is geared toward short-term work in an individual therapy setting. It is theory-based and supported by research on how to reliably, and with validity, infer units of information on review of videotapes and verbatim transcripts. The theory underlying this approach to understanding therapy is called **configurational analysis** (CA).

I developed CA as a complete theory, drawing from psychoanalytical theory, cognitive–behavioral theory, and interpersonal approaches. In this sense, it is a truly integrative theory. Drawing from psychodynamic approaches, CA emphasizes intrapsychic conflicts, defenses against awareness, and insight into obstacles to change. Drawing from cognitive–behavioral approaches, CA emphasizes the patient's information-processing style, **belief structure**, and behavioral avoidance patterns, as well as the importance of practicing new behaviors until they become relatively automatic alternatives to previous maladaptive choices. Drawing from interpersonal approaches, CA emphasizes self-schemas, relationship **schemas,** and interpersonal scripts and behaviors.

However, CA is also an original theory, developed by the author in the context of clinical investigation and described in more detail in several previous books written for researchers, theoreticians, and advanced psychotherapists (Horowitz, 1987, 1988b, 1991b, 1997, 1998; Horowitz et al., 1984b).

TERMINOLOGY

The triad of awareness, insight, and making new decisions about interpersonal behaviors is emphasized in this integration of theories. This triad is an idealized representation of the **cycles** of psychotherapy process (Figure 1). Most patients in short-term psychotherapy do not go through all the elements in this idealized depiction, but the image of the Figure may help clinicians think of what processes can happen to facilitate change.

Another triad to consider is a different threesome of interacting elements: states of mind, the controls of emotional processing and cognitive awareness that can change a person's states of mind, and the schemas of persons (self and others) that can organize each state. A concordance of states, controls, and person schemas with awareness, insight, and new decision is shown in Table 1.

Although some of these terms may now seem unfamiliar to most readers, they will come alive during the case presentation and discussion of the steps of CA. For those who wish to explore the theoretical and

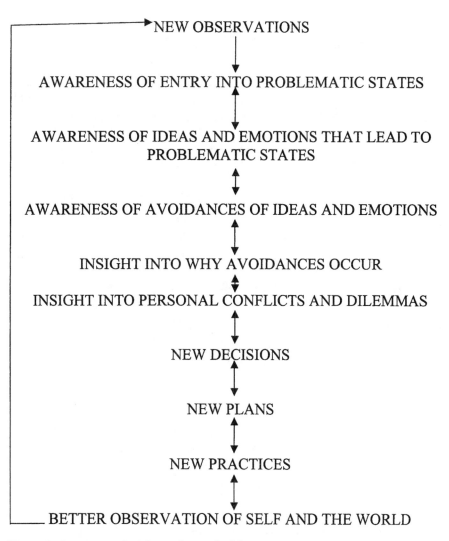

NEW OBSERVATIONS

↓

AWARENESS OF ENTRY INTO PROBLEMATIC STATES

↓

AWARENESS OF IDEAS AND EMOTIONS THAT LEAD TO
PROBLEMATIC STATES

↕

AWARENESS OF AVOIDANCES OF IDEAS AND EMOTIONS

↕

INSIGHT INTO WHY AVOIDANCES OCCUR

↕

INSIGHT INTO PERSONAL CONFLICTS AND DILEMMAS

↕

NEW DECISIONS

↕

NEW PLANS

↕

NEW PRACTICES

↕

BETTER OBSERVATION OF SELF AND THE WORLD

Figure 1. Awareness, insight, and new decisions.

research basis of this approach in more depth, see Horowitz (1998). However, for this volume to be a self-contained work, a brief overview of some of these theories and supporting research is discussed later. The reader will not need to read this background material, however, to understand and apply the steps of CA described in the remainder of the book. Some may wish to skip ahead because after this discussion, the organization of the book and how the steps of CA relate to the chapters of the book are described. This section of the introduction will help orient readers to the content and process of learning CA.

TABLE 1
States, Controls, and Person Schemas in Relation to Awareness, Insight, and Decision Making

	Awareness	Insight	Decision making
States	Knowing when a change in mood occurs	Understanding how and why a change in mood occurs	Planning how to avoid entry into dreaded or problematic states
Altering controls	Recognizing avoidance	Realizing how and why the avoidance occurs	Choosing to focus attention on and rework the warded-off topic
Person schemas	Knowing attributions of self and others	Finding differences between old fantasies and new opportunities	Choosing and rehearsing new roles and actions

THEORY AND RESEARCH

Research has been conducted on how to infer states of mind, cognitive–emotional themes, control of feelings, and enduring views that lead to variations in a sense of **identity** and relatedness.

State Analysis

In this book, **states** refers to both mental and behavioral patterns that seem in one individual recognizably different. A mood is a state but so are periods that seem flat and without any emotion.

State analysis is important in clinical work because it helps the clinician avoid static descriptions of people. A person can have both normal and abnormal states. Transient fluctuations from normal experiences to periods of delusional behavior, anxiety attacks, and multiple personalities in a single individual provided early impetus for state analyses (Gaarter, 1971).

Dissociative states have been described over 4,000 years of recorded history as prominent symptoms of what was once called *hysteria* (Vieth, 1977). These syndromes were explored in depth and explained in terms of unconscious roles, aims, fears, and defenses by Breuer and Freud in 1895 (1895/1957). Various states of consciousness, each characterized by styles of action and a predominance of particular ideas and feelings, were described for the person exhibiting hysterical phenomenon, an approach used in France by Charcot (1877) and Janet (1965). Breuer believed that the hypnoid state was of special etiological significance in the onset of hysterical symptoms.

The histrionic personality disorders (Horowitz, 1991a), as well as the narcissistic and borderline personality disorders (Hartocollis, 1977; Kernberg,

1975; Kohut, 1977), are characterized in part by the presence of sometimes-explosive shifts in state. State distinctions and cycles of change in a state can, however, be made by a clinician for any person. That is, a person's states and the smoothness or explosiveness of state transitions are the behavioral manifestations of his or her character structure.

Although flexibility in entering multiple states may be a sign of character strength, the inability to maintain a stable state may be a sign of character weakness (Horowitz, 1988a, 1998, 2002c; Kernberg, 1967). In individuals with unintegrated character formation, states may seem more diverse, sharply delineated, and unpredictably changing than those of individuals with more mature or harmonized levels of character development.

States that are common to most people include those periods dominated by expressions of emotion such as anxiety, anger, guilt, sadness, shame, sexual excitement, surprise, and joy. Each person experiences these general emotions in his or her own particular way. Each person may cry but each person has his or her own unique way of crying, emitting sounds, contorting facial muscles, experiencing sadness. Enormous work has been done on the general aspects of emotion, but little has been done to describe the unique variations experienced among individuals. In addition, there are states without much or any emotional expressivity.

Federn (1952) studied what he called ego states. In this instance, the word *ego* means self. Federn found evidence that the ego states of earlier developmental periods remained throughout life and were potentially recurrent in later behavior and experience. For example, an adult could regress to the ego states of childhood or adolescence. These might emerge during pathological or normal regressions.

Eric Berne (1961, 1964) built on Federn's work. He founded a school of therapy from a general theory of ego states and called it transactional analysis. He classified the general states of individuals as adult, child, and parent. Again, he was referring to self-states. It was his thesis that each person had within him- or herself these three characteristic roles for acting in the world and experiencing self and others. In any two-person system, such as a marriage or a love affair, there are six personifications in action: each party can be in a child, parent, or adult state.

For example, an adult-to-adult interchange between husband and wife might shift when the husband took on a parental role and addressed his wife as if she were a child, perhaps through criticism. If the wife enacted a dependent child role the marital state would be governed by a role-relationship model of husband as parent and wife as child. But another state, one of vindictive hostility, might ensue if the wife also entered a parental state and counterattacked the husband, criticizing him as if he were the wayward child. Both husband and wife would be "speaking down" to the other; in Berne's view, a state of domestic uproar would occur.

Continued work in the phenomenology of clinical psychology also indicated the necessity for describing multiple recurrent states for a given person. Bibring (1953) described the multiple states of the depressed person, and Kernberg (1975, 1984) is prominent among those who have shown the importance of describing different states and differing self–other roles for borderline patients and those with narcissistically vulnerable character. Both Kernberg (1975) and Mayman (1968) differentiated these multiple states according to the object relationships that organized self–other roles of each separate state.

My colleagues and I followed this early work of others. First, we established reliable methods for independent agreement when state transitions occurred on review of videotapes of psychotherapy. We found that judges could independently label the states that were observed between the transition points. Using a list of categorical descriptions of the states of a patient, judges who were clinicians or clinicians in training agreed significantly in statistical analyses of their ratings (Horowitz, Marmar, & Wilner, 1979; Marmar, Wilner, & Horowitz, 1984). Such research included validity studies: We found that problematic and uncontrolled states declined over the course of treatment.

Research on the reliability and validity of individualized state labeling can be done only one case at a time. When using a more general approach to characterizing types of states, across-subjects research becomes possible. We set out to find a useful, general list.

As already mentioned, emotionality is important when separating states into types. However, we found that it was more clinically useful to separate categories based on observed control of emotionality. By defining the degree of apparent self-governance of emotion, my colleagues and I were then able to show the reliability and validity of a general categorization of undermodulated, overmodulated, well-modulated, and shimmering states (which have discordant signs of both expressing and seeking to avoid expressing feelings; Horowitz, Milbrath, Ewert, et al., 1994).

Emotional and Cognitive Information Processing Theory and Research

The interaction between cognition, emotion, and the processes that regulate feeling states can be illustrated by considering how a person thinks over a stressor event after the event has ended. The memories and personal themes associated with the stressor event contain information that must be processed to realign beliefs and schemas with the present reality. Processing this topic evokes emotional responses. To prevent states that are too intense, a person controls consciously or unconsciously his or her rate or style of information processing. At the extreme, the topic is so avoided that it is never consciously contemplated or discussed, or else irrational distortions of meaning are introduced to ameliorate emotion.

When conscious information processing is interrupted, ideas are retained in some form of active memory outside of conscious awareness. Repugnant ideas may be preconsciously warded off, but they are not erased. Such active memories tend to be intrusively represented until fully processed (Horowitz, 1988a, 1988b, 2001, 2003). Even though the person attempts to prevent conscious expressions, such topics emerge unbidden and lead to pangs of unwanted emotion. Even if the topic does not return intrusively, warded-off ideas and memories may still influence actions without conscious recognition of such effects.

Suppose the stressor event is the death of a loved one. If rational information processing were to take place, the patient would appraise the loss of the loved one realistically and set new life goals, as needed, to cope immediately and eventually adapt well to the loss. The patient's inner models of self and relationship with the deceased would be changed to accord to the new external realities (Horowitz, 2001; Janis, 1969; Lazarus & Folkman, 1984). What makes the life event serious and stressful is the momentous difference between the patient's new realities on the one hand and the patient's inner model of attachments, intentions, and expectations with regard to the relationship to the deceased. This difference sets in motion processes directed at understanding all the implications of the loss, including new views of the self without the deceased in the future.

Contemplating the meanings of a dire event evokes strong negative emotion. These feelings can threaten the person with the unceasing possibility of entry into a dreaded, undermodulated state. To avoid such states, the person may block contemplation of them; this can act as an effective, dose-by-dose coping strategy or an obstacle to reaching eventual goals of completing a mourning process.

To repeat, the realization of a serious discrepancy between previous schemas and a new reality evokes emotions such as grief, panic, and anger. The potential of intense experience of these emotions is associated with a topic of concern. The possibility of intense, negative, and out of control emotional states can feel threatening. To avoid the danger of dreaded levels of feeling, the process of thinking consciously and communicating with others about such themes is regulated. Often, the patient has exercised such high inhibition that working through a conflicted topic has not yet occurred. The therapist acts to increase a sense of safety so that more emotional information processing occurs and leads to resolution of conflict.

A gradual and well-dosed approach involves a redeployment of controls. One can use voluntary and selective controls rather than involuntary and excessively global ones. One can model how to safely confront warded-off ideas and feelings. Each episode of contemplation then leads toward the goal of accommodation to the loss.

For example, in a patient who is suddenly bereaved, the loss and its implications are topics of concern. One can formulate how far this set of themes has been processed. In therapy, both patient and therapist seek to engage both topics that flood the patient with too much emotion and topics that are excessively warded off. Usually, intrusive topics are addressed first.

Although this book focuses on psychological factors, biological factors should be included whenever pertinent. For example, extreme fatigue, brain damage, or a toxic disturbance may render rational information processing impossible or working states unstable. Describing information processing in such an instance would include a statement of the cognitive operations the person could not perform, the maneuvers used as substitutes, and the capacities that remained intact. Social factors may also be relevant, as in societies in which certain types of thoughts or feeling states are forbidden according to a cultural code.

Clinically, formulating topics of concern and then noting the patient's entry into defensive states may signal which potentially important topics are currently active, emotionally arousing, and unresolved because of conflict (Horowitz, Milbrath, Jordan, et al., 1994).

The relevant scientific question is whether clinicians are so subjective that they cannot objectively discover and define key topics. In answer to this question research shows that clinicians can reliably identify conflicted topics. In quantitative studies, my colleagues and I reliably scored psychotherapy sessions, segmented transcripts, and videotapes for such topics. Using independent judges who were in clinical training, we also reliably scored and segmented for states such as shimmering. We also reliably scored specific verbal and nonverbal signs of defensive control of emotion (Horowitz, Kernberg, & Weinshal, 1993; Horowitz, Milbrath, Reidbord, & Stinson, 1993; Horowitz, Milbrath, & Stinson, 1995; Horowitz, Stinson, Curtis, et al., 1993; Horowitz, Stinson, Fridhandler, et al., 1993).

Clinically judged unresolved topics occurred most in temporal accord with reliably scored heightened signs of defensive emotional control. Verbal signs of such high control included efforts to retract and obscure statements already partially expressed, which is called dyselaboration. Nonverbal signs included contractions of the circular muscles around the eyes and mouth and aversion of the face from the therapist to conceal expressions of emotion. These findings support the validity of several steps of CA, especially its inclusion of some psychodynamic concepts of defensive layering of meanings and emotions.

Interpersonal Theories and Research

The most important schemas under consideration are those that are called person schemas. Schemas offer organized packaged views of the self and other people. A type of person schema is a role-relationship model. A role-relationship model is like a mental map or template of beliefs (or fantasies) about self and self within a specific type of relationship with inclusion of potential emotions and value judgments. This pattern includes scripts of interaction sequences that might take place, as well as characteristics of self and others. Schemas tend to endure once they have been formed but new variants can form as a consequence of recognizing and learning from new experiences (Bartlett, 1932; Horowitz, 1991a, 1998; Kagan, 1982; Piaget, 1937/1954; Stern, 1985). Formulating the dilemmas and contradictions in existing, enduring person schemas can provide a focus for therapy and an aim for what changes might be possible.

The assumptions that are key to CA are (a) that each individual has multiple self-concepts, which may or may not be integrated into supraordinate schemas; (b) that contradictory **configurations** of these multiple self-schemas and role-relationship models can lead to recurrent maladaptive state cycles; and (c) certain otherwise puzzling accretions of ideas within topics of concern can be unpacked by looking for such contradictions. To examine the issues of self-organization that are involved, some definitions are useful.

Person schemas may be activated when associated with the possibility of gratifying a wish or coping with a fear. They are used to interpret the present and plan the future, and they can also revise (perhaps erroneously) past memories. Freud, in his exploration of the Oedipus complex as a "family romance," exposed the unconscious persistence and dynamic power of early interpersonal relationship patterns throughout adult life (Freud, 1905, 1912/1955, 1912/1958). Jung's theory of the archetypes contained the idea of multiple, unconscious self-schemas (Stevens, 1982). Rapaport (1967), Arlow (1969), Kernberg (1975), and Knapp (1969) later elaborated on the unconscious, preconscious, and conscious layers of such relationship fantasies. Anna Freud (1936) continued Sigmund Freud's work in clarifying how defense mechanisms warded off not only specific memories and fantasies but dreaded self and object concepts as well.

Federn (1952) described how different states of behavior were associated with different self-feelings, findings elaborated on by Schilder (1950), Sullivan (1953), and Kohut (1971). Berne (1961) explained different ego states by way of different self-concepts as child, parent, or adult. Beck (1976), Beck and Emery (1985), and more recently Johnson (1994), Persons (1989), and Young and Mattila (2002) explored the schemas that might underlie repetitive and dysfunctional cognitions or beliefs. Categories for schemas and transactive tendencies have been developed from research on recurrent interpersonal patterns. These include polar dimensions for kindness to hostility, domination to subordination, and autonomy to dependence (Benjamin, 1979, 1993; Benjamin & Friedrich, 1991; Kiesler, 1983; Wiggins, 1979, 1982).

My own work on self-organization stemmed from studying the writings of the British Object Relations School (from Klein, 1948, to Bowlby, 1969, 1973, 1980), Erikson (1954), Hartmann (1950), Jacobson (1964), Kernberg (1975), Kohut (1971, 1977), Stern (1985), Sullivan (1953), and work on moral development summarized by Loevinger (1976). I attempted to clarify by careful case-by-case analysis the operation of multiple self-concepts, schemas, and role-relationship models in different states of mind as they were consciously and unconsciously operative (Horowitz, 1977, 1979, 1988a, 1991b, 1998; Horowitz & Zilberg, 1983).

I also studied and used the results of people who studied personality trait psychology. Kelly (1955), for example, developed a useful system by defining the core constructs a person habitually uses in appraisals of him- or herself and others. This led to considerable research on how interpersonal views are organized and indicated a fair degree of consciousness even about usually warded-off views (Bannister, 1985; Neimeyer, 1986).

The concept of person schemas operates across dynamic, cognitive–behavioral, cognitive science, and psychoanalytical schools of thought. The sequential schemas operating unconsciously when motivated are called core operating principles by Meichenbaum and Gilmore (1984). Markus (1977; Markus & Smith, 1981) has demonstrated that how people process information depends on the nature of their schemas for a given kind of trait. Berne (1964); Bower, Black, and Turner (1979); Carlson and Carlson (1984); Fiske and Taylor (1984); Kihlstrom and Cantor (1994); Schank and Abelson (1977); and Tomkins (1979) have provided work on how scripts operate preconsciously as organizing forms in social information processing. An integrated cognitive–psychodynamic point of view (Horowitz, 1998) adds motives, conflict between motives, and defensive regulation to these theories.

In a series of clinical studies, a configuration of desired, dreaded, and defensive schemas of self and other was developed. Inferences added patient-specific contents to a general format (Horowitz, 1979, 1988a, 1989; Horowitz et al., 1991). The next research effort examined the reliability of judges in matching psychotherapy videotapes to the configurations developed by other clinicians. Judges could do so with statistical significance, providing an indication of construct validity (Eells et al., 1995; Horowitz & Eells, 1993). The subsequent research involved having independent teams add patient-specific self-and-other relational concepts to this general format of a configuration of role-relationship models. Independent judges compared the results of two separate university teams and found satisfactory levels of consensus based on inference drawn from psychotherapy transcripts (Horowitz, Eells, Singer, & Salovey, 1995). Other studies confirmed that the procedures coordinated well and amplified other approaches to formulation (Horowitz, 1991b, 1997; Horowitz & Stinson, 1994; Horowitz, Stinson, & Milbrath, 1996; Horowitz, Znoj, & Stinson 1995; Eells et al., 1995).

STEPS OF CONFIGURATIONAL ANALYSIS AND ORGANIZATION OF THIS BOOK

Configurational analysis, as presented in this volume, consists of eight steps: Each step is explained and illustrated in separate chapters. Steps 1 through 4 focus on the initial case formulation and initial interventions. Steps 5, 6, and 7 allow for revising the case formulation and appropriate mid-course corrections to therapeutic interventions, as well as ongoing in-therapy evaluation of therapeutic outcome. Step 8 finalizes the evaluation of therapeutic outcome.

The steps are illustrated using a key illustrative example, a patient I have called Janice. Janice was in her mid-20s when she entered psychotherapy, and her therapy involved age-appropriate developmental issues of the kind frequently presented in individual psychotherapy. Throughout the volume, selected transcripts will illustrate key points; certain features have been changed.[1] Quoted passages essentially reflect her own wording.

Key terms are set in boldface type and defined as they first appear, and these definitions will be repeated in the glossary at the end of the book.

CA is a systematic method. The system has been found to be useful in application to many kinds of patient and therapist situations, including different emphases on what is key to effective psychotherapy. The reason it works well is that it is more form than content. You, the therapist, provide the contents of each step based on your observations and inferences about your particular patient. I present the system from surface toward depth. Keep in mind that (a) you can change the form to more closely fit you and your patient, and (b) the contents you put in the form are never "all there is" or "the deepest roots"; the contents will not necessarily occur to you in the order of the CA system. Many of us find in doing Step 4, for example, we get an "aha!" of recognition about what we can then put in Steps 1, 2, or 3. Be open to these epiphanies!

---

[1] The actual patient gave informed consent to her interviews being recorded and to the use of her records for teaching and research purposes. The case has been in part fictionalized and generally simplified for generality and didactic ease.

I

CASE FORMULATION

1

JANICE'S CASE AND STEPS 1 THROUGH 4

The following example of a patient in short-term psychotherapy illustrates initial case formulation and beginning therapeutic process using a configurational analysis (CA) approach. As noted in the introduction, this case will be used throughout chapters 1 through 8.

PRECIPITATING CRISIS

Janice was a 24-year-old college graduate who complained of depressed moods when she sought short-term psychotherapy from the author (who is an older man). Janice's depressive moods had intensified after her younger brother was diagnosed with a potentially fatal illness, a form of difficult-to-treat cancer that sometimes strikes young adults. In the initial evaluation interview, Janice stated that she felt unable to feel her emotions; she said she feared she might "fall apart." She also said that she was "unable to get herself together" during the months that followed her brother's diagnosis.

When Janice came home from work one day, several months after her brother's diagnosis, she was informed by Phillip, her domestic partner, that a call had come in stating her brother had lost consciousness and had been hospitalized in an unstable condition. She felt initial disbelief—"It's a prank call"—and countered her reaction by saying, "But it can't be a joke." Then she immediately focused her attention on practical arrangements such as making a reservation for the airplane trip home. "Right away, I started avoiding it, cried only a little, and shifted to an intellectual plane to ward off tears."

In addition to describing an "inability to emotionally confront the possibility of losing her brother" and the fear that she might fall apart, she told the clinician that she was concerned that her responses after her brother's hospitalization might interfere with her performance on her recently acquired job. She reported that reminders of her brother triggered intrusive fears that he might soon die. She had a few nightmares related to death and dreams of her family that she could not recall in detail. Otherwise, she had intrusive or "floating thoughts" about her relationship with her ill brother "with no feelings attached." She had, however, been worried by fantasies of her boyfriend dying.

She described periodic states of depression before the crisis. These moods had increased in frequency since her brother's hospitalization. During these dull, apathetic states Janice reported feeling lazy and sulky and worried about "constantly failing" in relationships with men and with her mother. Because of the increase in these states of depression, she was in danger of losing her job because on some workdays she stayed home, retreated to her bed, "indulging" herself in amusements that required "no thought," because at such times "any thought is dangerous."

The sudden onset of her brother's illness and subsequent hospitalization contributed to a sense that the occurrences were unreal. Additional fantasies were compensatory daydreams, which seemed to serve the aim of denial. When Janice reflected on these fantasies, she knew that they had no basis in reality, and when she thought logically, they made no sense to her.

Janice returned to her family's home during her brother's sudden hospitalization and after, and spent a total of 2 weeks with her family. The whole visit was fraught with family conflict. She and her younger siblings treated the hospitalization as a normal part of curing her brother's condition. This was not realistic, and they knew it. Yet the younger generation was angered with efforts by the older family members, especially their parents, to regard the hospitalization for what it was: a sign of her brother's deteriorating condition, and "turned it into a prelude to dying and a funeral." Janice, the eldest sibling, served as a "leader against family solidarity" around the issue of how normal and how seriously the hospitalization should be viewed. She was chastised by her mother for "fooling around and being silly."

At home while her brother was still in the hospital, Janice avoided visitors who came to support the family. She withdrew upstairs to rest on her bed and "avoid her mother's tears" and the "special attention" her mother received by being comforted by friends. She alternated between feelings of disgust at her mother's emotional display and a kind of envious admiration of her mother's ability to cry and "stay in bed." Her ill brother had always been Janice's favorite sibling because she said he admired and praised her rebellious independence and sibling leadership during her adolescence. Nonetheless, she felt "my role wasn't chief mourner, by any means; that was mother's role."

Her father also criticized Janice for "acting weird" during her visit. She felt quite vulnerable because she did not cry at the hospital and withdrew upstairs whenever friends and relatives came to the house. She felt angry and disgusted—"I was a square peg in a round hole." She maintained her distance from the family tradition of tears and a unified front even in the face of her mother's pleas that "this is not the time to be independent, at least now behave yourself!" She had feelings of wanting "unqualified" love from her mother instead of criticism. She wanted to leave soon after her brother had been stabilized in the hospital and released. She was irritated when her mother urged her to stay at home with the family not only for a few more days but for good. This would, she believed, in effect end her striving for independence. One reason she had moved 1,000 miles away was to keep her distance.

HISTORY

Janice was the eldest of several siblings raised in an intact, middle-class family. She had no history of a previous diagnosis of a psychiatric disorder but had twice sought counseling in the past in school settings. In high school, Janice saw a counselor for a few sessions based on conflicts related to dating. She again sought counseling in her college student health center after she "fell apart" following the end of a 1-year love relationship. She "missed the whole spring" of that academic year because of difficulty making herself study.

Janice described her father as stable and caring but unable to express emotion. According to her, he felt successful in his work as a union officer. He expected Janice to obtain good grades, engage in important activities, and achieve "golden" popularity. She saw her mother as a constant, committed housewife who had married at an early age and looked for gratification through raising her children. She felt her mother had shown "qualified and conditional love" when she said, "I want you to be happy," but meant, "I want you to be what I want you to be."

Janice saw her parents' relationship as interdependent but conflicted. Her mother turned to Janice as a "confidante" and expressed feelings of subordination, sexual frustration, and low self-esteem. Her father took many side trips for his workers' union with no consideration of a vacation for the family. Mother invariably seemed to submit to her husband's expectations.

She was overweight, Janice thought, because she turned to food for comfort, a pattern she fostered in her children. Her mother felt her life was "lost," that she should never have married her husband. Janice felt pushed by her mother to make the same choices: "I have to live her life to prove it was worth her having done it."

Although denying sibling rivalry, Janice admitted she always felt "special" compared with her siblings. She was the oldest and "the only girl for a long time," even though she was only a little over a year old when her brother, now ill, was born. She felt some guilt for always "outshining" this next-younger brother. She globally recalled a "happy, happy childhood." Play with girlfriends alternated with withdrawal to solitary reading. Her father would then tease and admonish her to go out and play. Janice and her siblings were characterized as "rebellious . . . we've all given them (parents) as much trouble as we could." She recalled various restrictions placed on her during adolescence. Even though the school permitted it, she was prohibited from going to high school in sandals, because such behavior would reflect badly on her mother.

Janice had a particular conflict with her parents around her sexuality and their strict, religious, and conventional morality. As soon as her mother discovered that she engaged in and, perhaps worse, enjoyed sexual relationships, "we've been fighting in that area ever since." Her mother stated that women should not have sexual intimacy until marriage and accused the patient, who did not agree, of being a "nymphomaniac and slut."

Her teachers told Janice that she had high IQ scores. To Janice, these scores suggested relative underachievement, "a lot of potential I never lived up to." She completed college while living at home and, after graduation, moved far away from her family in an effort to become more independent. She majored in music and took courses in composition but did not practice her instrument after college.

Work experience, since her move away from her family, had a quality of "underemployment." She characterized her job as "flunky's work." Although dissatisfied, she felt that her job as a low-paid caretaker at a home for the elderly was "safe . . . not too challenging." Her work conflicts emerged gradually throughout this and later sessions.

Although initially insistent about the absence of any "homesickness" for family or friends, she later acknowledged that "functioning on her own" during the past year had been difficult. Family pressures to return home continued, but she resisted. Her stated future plans were that she would return to school for an advanced degree with an ultimate wish to marry "for the title, legitimacy, and status."

Aside from Phillip, a lover with whom she had lived for the past 3 months, Janice had few friends; she had only one close woman friend in another part of the country. Her feelings remained "foggy" concerning

Phillip. Her previous boyfriend in college was "intellectual, verbal, and dazzled me." Phillip was described as less intelligent, but sensitive, attractive, and "he pays attention to me." But she also saw him as similar to her father, sometimes unresponsive to her. She found this frustrating—"It makes me feel worthless." Although considering the relationship "in flux . . . not an established thing," she suspected that she was "using him for security . . . the one-room apartment is like a womb . . . he accepts me." Before coming to therapy she had begun to feel that she ought to break up with him and move on.

Since her brother's hospitalization, Janice had feared losing Phillip, likening him to an "underdog" (as she had viewed her brother). At one point, she had a fantasy of Phillip's death through "brain disease" and imagined herself crying at his funeral. In that fantasy, the funeral was also attended by his ex-woman friend, who was competing for the position of "chief mourner" (similar to feelings related to her mother during her brother's hospitalization). Such fantasies were associated with fears of being alone and "vegetating." Janice felt that she might be unable to establish a new relationship because of her perceived tendency to "suck everything out of a relationship . . . demand and demand until the poor guy breaks." She drew parallels with "a friend" who is in a "bad relationship out of fear of not getting anyone else."

Patient's Attitude to Therapy

Janice's initial expectations regarding therapy were that she would be unable to "feel" in therapy. She was afraid that she would impress the therapist with her intelligence but would be unable to get in touch with and resolve her authentic feelings. Janice feared that the work in therapy might end her relationship with Phillip, once she "looked at it clearly." She was also afraid that therapy would make her "worse." She questioned whether she really wanted to experience "the feelings." She was concerned that she would become dependent on the therapist. Recording of the therapy for research and teaching purposes appealed to her. She thought she would be of service to the world and a potential audience would protect her from being dominated or misused by the therapist.

Patient's Self-Description

Janice had always wanted to be a composer and believed that she should have written her first sonata by the age of 17. Now it was "too late." She was a "snob about status" and "should be a symphony conductor," although she procrastinated whenever she thought of actions related to developing additional skills for playing or composing music.

In addition to underachieving and "fearing failure," Janice viewed herself as never experiencing authentic feelings; she would "act open," while being secretive, or behave like a "modern woman" while feeling like "giving up" and becoming "an asexual old lady." She thought that her body image was sometimes "ugly-disgusting." She felt like she had no "will power," preferring to "control things to the extent of wanting to know all the details about things before they happen." Interpersonal relationships were colored by her feelings of greed (to the extent of referring to herself as a "vampire") and by her efforts to manipulate others into complimenting her or feeling sorry for her. If Janice was successful at getting pity, she felt contempt for the person fooled into offering it. She felt like a failure when relationships ended but entered them with the covert self-statement, "Here I am, totally worthless; love me anyway, and I'll think less of you if you do."

Therapist's Initial Description of the Patient

The patient was alert and appropriately dressed. She communicated by using many facial expressions and hand movements for additional dramatic emphasis but maintained a fixed smile beneath that seemed affectively flat. Her voice was strained with lapses into sounding childlike when talking of her mother. She often spoke abstractly when questioned. She appeared to be keeping emotions at a distance by being vague. She also appeared to be using denial and intellectualization, as she would shift between topics or shift her attitudes on a given topic in an unemotional way.

INITIAL FORMULATION: STEPS 1 THROUGH 4 OF CONFIGURATIONAL ANALYSIS

I am now going to cover the main dimensions of CA. First, I will go through the four steps about phenomena, states, topics, and schemas of self and others. These beginning instructions will be brief and general. I will then go through them again in more detail, using more examples from the case of Janice. Gradually, by repetition, a beginning clinician may get these dimensions in mind, as a format for use in formulating cases.

Step 1: Phenomena to Be Explained

The first step is to list salient phenomena. In undertaking Step 1, the clinician lists phenomena that can be observed (signs) or reported (symptoms and problems). Phenomena also include inabilities and repetitive maladaptive actions, as well as distressing experiences. Because we have just reviewed the material presented in the early phase of Janice's short-term therapy, we

EXHIBIT 1.1
Phenomena for Janice at Onset of Therapy

Symptoms

Several years of "depressions" characterized by apathy, withdrawal, feeling foggy and unreal, overeating, and feelings of self-disgust.

Signs

Remote from direct and emotional communication with therapist.

Problems in living

Episodically unable to motivate self to work, leading to fear of losing her job.
Sometimes too dependent, dramatic, or disingenuous.
Wants to be more creative.
Desires more affiliated relationships with both sexes.

---

can look at how the problems were initially listed by the therapist (see Exhibit 1.1). Later these are compared as they were formulated over time and assessed as treatment outcomes. I will now, and in successive steps, put in display type instructions you may wish to review again later on.

> Select and describe the symptoms, problems, and maladaptive personality traits that need to be explained. One can discuss this selection with the patient: Does he or she agree on the importance of trying to change particular symptoms, problems, or traits? With some patients this helps to establish an initial focus for further discourse.

Step 2: States of Mind

In Step 2, the clinician describes states of mind in which these phenomena do and do not occur. An initial configuration of states uses a psychodynamic triangle of the patient's wishes, fears, and defensive compromises between approach and avoidance motives. That is, the clinician may formulate cycles of shifting moods that involve the emotionality of desired, dreaded, and defensive compromise states.

Some beginners find this task daunting. However, those I have supervised find satisfaction when they start with a case and list what they know or infer without striving for perfection, and then make several passes through the steps as they become more familiar with the method. State **analysis** is important and is the main aspect of CA that has been missing from purely cognitive–behavioral approaches to formulation. Elements in a problem list and dysfunctional cognitions are not invariable: They may vary qualitatively as well as quantitatively in a person's different but repetitive states.

> Describe states in which the selected phenomena do and do not occur, as well as recurrent maladaptive cycles of states. Organize these when possible into configurations of desired states, dreaded states, and

EXHIBIT 1.2
States for Janice: A First Approximation

1. Hurt and not working	She appears insulated or aloof, stops tasks, withdraws.
2. Hurt but working	She seems deflated but goes on with her tasks.
3. Tra-la-la	She is cheerful, lighthearted, entertaining, pretending.
4. Depressed?	Unclear, may be like hurt and not working.

compromise states. Compromise states can be divided into those that are more problematic and those that are more protective. When appropriate, the therapist can discuss with the patient his or her states of mind. The patient can then join the formulation process and increase his or her self-monitoring skills. This may clarify the motives used to avoid negative emotional states that feel out of control. Such conversations help the clinician to ascertain the patient's skills at self-observation.

As mentioned, I am using display type to provide a reader with a quick method for thumbing back to these instructions for a step of CA. That may help one use this system for formulating personal cases. As for Janice, Exhibit 1.2 illustrates the therapist's first approximation of what he observed initially. As mentioned before, more detail is presented in the next chapter. For now, let us just go on to the next step.

Step 3: Topics of Concern and Defensive Control Processes

Problematic and dreaded states usually contain unwanted ideas and feelings. In Step 3, one looks for important topics that generate distressing emotionality or constrictive defenses. This effort at lucid inferences about unresolved topics of concern is continued in Step 4, which identifies the views of self and others as well as key motives, values, and expectations that are found to organize each of the patient's different states of mind.

The ebb and surge of thinking or communicating or being reminded of topics of concern often explain, in part, why shifts in states occurs. Additional explanation later, in Step 4, adds to understanding.

Describe situations, stimuli, and topics of concern that may trigger entry into dreaded and problematic states. Describe how expressions of ideas and emotions are obscured. Infer how emotionally stifled states function to ward off close encounters with the unresolved topics. Describe habitual styles of controlling emotion and impulse. Describe how shifts in **defensive control processes** lead to a change of state and to movement through a state cycle. Discuss patterns of topic avoidance with the patient to clarify resistances and obstacles to treatment. Discuss the

EXHIBIT 1.3
**Initial Approximation of Topics of Concern and
Defense Control Processes for Janice**

Topic 1. The serious illness of her brother and what it means to her. She interrupts contemplation of this probably to ward-off intense grief and fear for stability of self.

Topic 2. Dilemma of whether to return home or stay in present location (also related to career and relationship choices). She seems to ward-off possible shame over self-centered behaviors by blaming her mother. She may also ward off longing for her mother and rage at her by intellectualizations and topic avoidances.

concept that therapy engages highly charged topics in a dose-by-dose manner rather than an overwhelming single episode.

An approximation of initial inferences about Janice by therapist is shown in Exhibit 1.3.

Step 4: Identity and Relationships

Identity sensations and relationship beliefs, patterns of action, and interpersonal emotionality are not static. They shift. They both evoke and are evoked by changeable moods. Yet patterns can be observed.

Each state of mind may have its own organizing schemas of self and how self articulates with the world, especially the world of relationships. Each person may have several **self-schemas** as well as a repertoire of self as transacting with significant types of people. These cognitive maps of self and other contain emotional potentials. That is why this is a deeper level of inference than the first three steps. Because of this depth this step will usually be sketchy and incomplete early in therapy. It can be revised during the process of treatment.

Describe organizing roles, beliefs, and scripts of expression in each state. Describe wish–fear dilemmas in relation to desired and dreaded role-relationship models. Infer how defensive control processes may activate compromise role-relationship models that ward off dangers and lead to problematic and protective compromise states. Identify dysfunctional attitudes and how these are involved in maladaptive state cycles. Consider whether to discuss with the patient the self-images and roles in important relationships that you infer to be problematic. If you do, clarify agreements, disagreements, and motivations for change. This will help select foci for joint attention.

These instructions are a tall order for beginning therapists in initial sessions. All that is needed, however, is a first approximation. It may or

EXHIBIT 1.4
An Approximation of the Recurrent Self–Other Concepts
Initially Presented by Janice

1. *Desired state:* Self as a competent, engaging woman seeking a competent companion and feeling potential satisfaction, safety, and security.
2. *Tra-la-la state:* Self as an as-if competent woman fooling a competent companion by pretending and so feeling both vulnerable and aloof.
3. *Hurt and not working state:* Self as a needy person unable to get or keep a good, caring relationship and so feeling confusing medley of fear, anger, sadness, shame, and guilt.

may not be possible to do something such as outlined in Exhibit 1.4 for Janice. More will be possible as more time for observation and understanding occurs.

In taking process notes of therapy hours it is often useful to include (after a first summary) these same categories: phenomena, states, topics, and self–other concepts or schemas. Consider making a form with these headings and blank spaces. Just pop any relevant inference into each category. Tolerate the inevitable blank or ambiguous spaces, because formulation is a gradual modifying process.

CONCLUSION

Perhaps a reader will not feel satisfied with this overview of Steps 1 through 4 as a prelude to doing CA with personal patients. If so, because this overview was meant to be a synopsis, please do not worry. Each step is covered again in more depth in the chapters that follow.

2

STEPS 1 AND 2: DESCRIBING
PHENOMENA AND STATES OF MIND

Before describing Steps 1 and 2 in more detail, it might be helpful to look at the work with Janice in terms of a chronology of sessions 1 through 4. This will give a better feel for the actual in vivo therapy process as a prelude to the therapist's out-of-session configurational analysis (CA) work on formulation.

At the first session, Janice presented herself to the therapist as if at ease, but she seemed tense. She told the story about her brother's illness and described her anger at various authority figures involved in his diagnosis, sudden hospitalization, and its aftermath. She said she tended to use news of his status as having a terminal disease mainly to get sympathy for herself; she was not experiencing the sadness that she thought was deep within her. The therapist felt that there was a diffusion of focus and that Janice struggled against his efforts to establish focus on her reactions to the potential loss of her brother. Logistical arrangements for a once-a-week, individual, time-limited therapy were easily settled.

The second session focused on her resistances to frank discourse in therapy sessions, especially her apparent need to avoid being degraded by exposure of feelings and private ideas. The therapist observed that she seemed emotionally disengaged from the ideas she communicated. He asked her to recollect aspects of how she reacted to news about her brother and the ensuing events such as going home after his hospitalization. There was no emotional response to these topics; however, she came close to tears later in the hour when the therapist said that now that she had left home, she was on new paths in her life that would lead her toward what she wished to become. After this intervention, she said she was yearning to develop a close friendship with a woman but had few promising connections.

At the beginning of the third session, Janice seemed more pressured, even though she put on a jolly front. The interview focused on her relationship with her parents, especially their criticism of her lifestyle. Her father was more overtly critical; he told her that she was stupid for living with a person like Phillip. Her mother, although basically more covert in her criticism, had accused Janice of being a nymphomaniac and urged her to act more like her. Other topics included reactions to the initial news of the brother's illness, his subsequent hospitalization, and a hint of some unsatisfactory events surrounding it. No details were given. A new problem emerged; she was close to being fired from her work because of difficulties with her supervisor.

The therapist asked for concrete episodes of difficulties she experienced with her work supervisor, with Phillip, as well as with her mother and father. There was some focus on the therapy itself, on how the goals and focus seemed diffuse. The therapist posited that Janice may have used the circumstances of her brother's illness as a ticket of admission to therapy that she wanted for other meaningful but unclarified reasons. Janice did not arrive for the next scheduled session. The therapist called and rescheduled.

In the fourth session, there was discussion about the hour she had missed without calling the previous week. The session was scheduled on the day of her birthday and she had been depressed. Instead of keeping her appointment, she had stayed home and cried. She said she called to cancel but no message was left for the therapist. In this session, she was more depressed than in any previous session and seemed on the verge of quitting.

Content in this session also revolved around how she was treated unfairly at the home for the elderly where she worked and felt like the lowest person there. The therapist said that she provoked the criticism by behaving at work in a passive–aggressive manner. When she felt hurt by this, the therapist said that she felt insulted by his remark. She was able to acknowledge that this was so.

We return to these hours later. For the moment it is useful to note that Janice is emotionally avoidant as well as distressed. She came for reasons that become unclear after therapy started. In such instances a systematic and gradual approach to case formulation is especially useful.

Step 1: Phenomena to Be Explained

Although a patient's chief complaints are paramount, a useful list of problems that need explaining in the course of formulation includes additional information. A good clinician, especially in brief therapy, needs to select from an often perplexing array of problems. I begin a problem list with patient-stated symptoms, as well as signs of possible **psychopathology** that I observe. Then I add the problems in living that the patient might be experiencing, which are often not quite symptoms or signs. Some patients, for example, complain of anxiety and depressive symptoms and then reveal how they are impaired at work, in intimate social relationships, or in caring for their children. I sometimes find it useful to add to this list of phenomena to be examined, a patient's thwarted goals and decisional quandaries.

In case formulation, the therapist should avoid the common obstacles of being too fussy, compulsive, or perfectionistic. This is a messy, ambiguous, and often confusing business. Clarity comes eventually: Just start somewhere. Then you can add, erase, and revise.

In terms of clinical phenomena, do not expect to know everything relevant during your first meeting with a patient. Begin a list, then change it as observations emerge in later sessions. Patients often come with complaints that are either shaped by previous clinician interviews, well-meaning confidants, or their own beliefs and fantasies about what will serve as a kind of ticket-of-admission to your services or to insurance coverage. With trust in your empathy and expertise, they may revise their understanding and reveal what motivates them to seek a process of personal restoration or developmental change.

The steps of formulation include a description of problematic states and unresolved emotional topics. Do not attempt categorical exclusiveness: You can list a topic or state as a relevant phenomenon and then repeat it when you go on to the next two steps that describe in more depth states and topics. For example, if a patient says she sometimes has states in which she is troubled by hostile impulses toward her baby, that goes to the head of the list of phenomena. Then, in the next step, on state analysis, there may be listed a state of potentially violent rage as well as states when anger or frustrations are less volatile. Under Step 3, on topics of concern, you will again describe the theme as a topic of being concerned over having, perhaps, a reaction of resentment at the baby for making what seems like insatiable demands. This is fleshed out more thoroughly in Step 4, where roles attributed to the baby and mother in states that are hostile, loving, and indifferent to caretaking are elaborated.

Some patients present, as a complaint, topics of concern that are difficult for them to resolve. Add these to the list of phenomena. For

EXHIBIT 2.1
The Early Phenomena List for Janice

Symptoms
Several years of "depressions" characterized by apathy, withdrawal, feeling foggy and unreal, overeating, and feelings of self-disgust.

Signs
Remote from direct and emotional communication with therapist.

Problems in living
Episodically unable to motivate self to work, leading to fear of losing her job.
Sometimes too dependent, dramatic, or disingenuous.
Wants to be more creative.
Desires more affiliated relationships with both sexes.

example, a patient may report a sense of blocked grief for a relative who has been dead for years. A goal of that patient may be to complete mourning. Just list "sense of incomplete mourning." Of course, this issue will be repeated later as a topic of concern.

As for Janice as our case example, we already made an early list of phenomena and Exhibit 1.1 is reproduced here as Exhibit 2.1 so we can face it onto a page showing a revision, which is Exhibit 2.2. Exhibit 2.2 is just a bit different. It could have been done at the end of the four beginning sessions summarized at the beginning of this chapter. The organizational headings of Exhibit 2.2 are a little different than in Exhibit 2.1. This is only to show that there is no need for rigidity: Do this step in a way that fits your approach, with your patient. The point is to clarify what you will be dealing with and trying to explain in the next steps of CA.

Step 2: States of Mind

State description is a way of condensing the therapist's multiple observations into a limited set of patterns. Because a person can exhibit many details of behavior, a selective process is needed. It is often helpful to begin state description with states that contain symptomatic phenomena. After listing these problematic states, list the states that regulate affect. One will often find that one has then described undermodulated states, states that seem more in control, and those that seem overcontrolled to others and then may feel inauthentic in the privacy of the patient's own mind.

Maladaptive repetitive interpersonal patterns often involve a cycle of several states. To recognize such maladaptive cycles, one begins by noting frequent state transitions into and out of a problematic state. Then one can discuss these states according to their motivational and defensive arrange-

EXHIBIT 2.2
Phenomena for Janice: A Later Look

Complaints

1. Specific: not reacting properly to potentially fatal illness of brother.
2. General: several years of "depressions" characterized by apathy, withdrawal, feeling foggy and unreal, overeating, feelings of self-disgust.

Additional problems

1. Problems with self: episodically unable to motivate self to work, leading to fear of losing job.
2. Problems with others: sometimes too competitive, negative, passive–aggressive, dependent, dramatic, or disingenuous.
3. Remorseful over her behavior at returning home because of brother's illness.

Formulated problems

1. Incomplete emotional reaction to stress of brother's illness with denial of strong component of felt damage to self because of impending loss.
2. Negative and defective self-images defended against by a kind of as-if role playing of positive self-images.
3. Unresolved attachment to mother with ambivalent identification; aims for independence in conflict with a desire for dependence.

ments. Even a problematic state can seem preferable to a more dreaded state, just as tension may be preferable to total despair. Also, consider what unachievable states are desired. Sometimes achieving more satisfaction can reduce dreaded states of despair.

WHAT IS A STATE?

A state is a recurrent pattern of experience, mood, and behavior that is both verbal and nonverbal in its manifestations. States are commonly recognized during a clinical interview because the patient may change his or her gesture, bodily stance, facial expression, intonation, or inflection of speech. Patients may also report differences from state to state in their self-image, mood, clarity of thought, empathy for others, and other internal mental qualities.

The states of a particular person are as easy to recognize in everyday life as is the change of atmosphere in a drama from light to dark or in music from a major to a minor mode. A state description may include the patient's patterns in posture, facial expression, tone of voice, gestures, style of speech, dialect, deployment of gaze, and other physical signs of attention focus. These manifestations will often convey the emotional coloration of a given state of mind. The therapist may include the patient's report of the specific topics as well as their felt emotions as labeled in their own words or described in their own images, similes, or metaphors.

The congruence or discord between verbal and nonverbal emotional colorations is important. Some states have a discrepancy between the type of mood conveyed in physical expression and that which is reported verbally: They are called shimmering states (as introduced earlier). In shimmering states such discords are what are centrally observed.

Each person has many states. State examination during CA requires a selection of those that are most relevant. Four to eight are usually sufficient. These states can be described and then given a brief label. By labeling a state, one has a name for a kind of experience. For example, a state of "towering and violent rage" is not the same as a state of "simmering vexation." Labels then serve as tools for discussing states; they allow for better contemplation by both patient and therapist so that additional observations can be made. The language of referring to different states can often be useful in discourse with patients; it may help them in their task of improving their self-observation.

In self-analysis, one can find a name for one's own states. Try this. One can ask one's domestic partner, family member, or close friend to describe one's states. In **psychotherapy,** both patient and therapist may name a state.

How each state feels to the patient, or how it is experienced by another person can be described in general terms of being in or out of control of emotionality. It can also be described motivationally as a desired or dreaded state. Such descriptions add dynamic qualities to the observed pattern of ideas, emotions, and particular behaviors that characterize each state. That is, one state can be stabilized to prevent entry into a more dreaded state.

State labels are derived from the prominent qualities that impress the subject or the viewer. These labels often stem from the prominent emotions and their degree of apparent or felt self-control, as well as their reactions of wanting to have or avoid the state. For example, a prevailing apparent mood can be happiness, but a state may also have an as-if or pretending quality. We learn socially now to pretend well-being. One patient called such a state "happy face" because she put on the face of happiness for others while inwardly feeling more theatrical than real.

This was a protective and overcontrolled state. It was used to protect her from entry into a dreaded state she called "terrible misery," in which she felt out of control and manifested undermodulated emotions that made her feel ashamed. Happy face was better, and in the direction of what she wanted, but it was not a desired state of well-modulated satisfaction with life in which she could feel and act authentically.

As already mentioned, emotionality is important when separating states into types, such as anxious, depressed, and resentful moods. However, we found that it was more clinically useful to separate categories based on observed control of emotionality. Well-modulated hostility is quite different from undermodulated hostility. By defining the degree of apparent self-control of emotion, my colleagues and I were then able to show the reliability and validity of a general categorization of undermodulated, overmodulated, well-modulated, and shimmering states (Horowitz, Milbrath, Ewert, et al., 1994).

Undermodulated states include impulsive actions and unregulated displays of feeling; expressions of emotion can seem explosive, blatant, or raw. Pangs of feeling that are usually restrained can erupt and lead to unwelcome action. Fear and anxiety are often added to a central experience, such as that of extreme rage, because the patient has a sense of losing control.

During **overmodulated states,** people appear excessively restrained or rigid. They maintain a poker face, pretend unfelt attitudes, or manifest indifference to friendly empathy. Some banter or buffoonery can seem overmodulated. An inability to shift out of an overmodulated state into a spontaneous, intimate, engaging kind of state impairs one's ability to love and work well; it explains many rigid aspects of personality, such as traits of woodenness with lack of passion or creative sparkle.

In **well-modulated states,** a relatively harmonious accord across modes of expression is observed. The person feels and appears to be in self-control, even when expressing intense, distressing emotions and troublesome ideas.

Some states combine several qualities of emotional modulation. That is, **shimmering states** combine features of what might otherwise be several states. These states have an oscillating and discordant pattern of elements. For example, leakage of emotional expression alternates rapidly with efforts to suppress it: The person may tear up, smile, and talk of something remote from sadness. A feeling expressed in a facial movement may also discord with the emotionality conveyed in words and vocal tone. One notices the quick shuffling of contradictory expressions, verbal and nonverbal (see Exhibit 2.3).

Overmodulated states can serve as a defense against a transition into anticipated dreaded, undermodulated states. For example, some disturbed patients know they have an unwanted, involuntary tendency to enter into undermodulated states that are characterized by irrational impulses based on delusional beliefs. Often such patients try to prevent transition into such states by using an overmodulated state characterized by irony, mockery, sarcasm, and facetiousness. They rigidly control impulses and show instead a heightened display of social decorum that can reach the point of absurdity.

EXHIBIT 2.3
Control of Emotion: Regulatory States With General Definitions

Undermodulated states	Undermodulated states appear to the observer as though the individual has dysregulation of emotional expression. This leads to appraisals of the individual as impulsive, uncontrolled, or experiencing intrusive concepts and emotions. Sharp increases in intensity of expression may suddenly appear as the individual experiences flares, surges, or pangs of emotion. The observer may experience a surge of emotion as an empathic response or perhaps feel a wish to intervene in a way that will help the patient regain control.
Well-modulated states	Well-modulated states exemplify a relatively smooth flow of expression. Affective displays appear genuine and, regardless of intensity, are expressed in a poised manner. The observer may feel subjective interest and empathy, with a sense of being connected to the individual and the material presented. The observer appraises the individual as engaged in an organized process of communication without major discords between verbal and nonverbal modes of expression.
Overmodulated states	Overmodulated states are characterized by excessive control of expressive behavior. The individual seems stiff, enclosed, masked, or walled off. To the observer, the individual's emotional displays—if present—may seem feigned or false. The observer appraises the individual as being distant from genuine communication. Therefore, the observer may feel disconnected from the individual, even bored or inattentive.
Shimmering states	Shimmering states are characterized by the individual shifting rapidly between undercontrolled emotions and overcontrolled emotion. The observer may recognize discordant signs of expression in verbal and nonverbal modes. The clashing signals may occur simultaneously or within a brief period of time.

They might hesitantly act, interrupt the action, and then act very slowly, only to interrupt it again (Sass, 1992).

STATE ANALYSIS WITH PATIENTS

In clinical work, state analysis can become a useful joint venture. Most patients know when they have changes in state. But they often have no language for making apt distinctions. The psychotherapist helps them arrive at a clear description and then a label for each state. A personal name for an experienced state in and of itself is a step toward a sense of developing more conscious control.

Of course, the clinician may be ahead of the patient, naming states for use in his or her own case formulation. However, it is often helpful to use the patient's words whenever possible. Later on, states are examined in discourse with the patient. Joint labels can then be used to (a) help the patient to better observe and report observe self-states, (b) describe cyclic patterns to the therapist, and (c) control a potential transition into an unwanted state.

Experience is the teacher for therapists. At first, trainees find it somewhat difficult to observe states. The reason for this is that they focus on stories that the patient tells and wonder a lot about what they can do to help right away. With effort, state observation becomes easier, enhancing intuition as well as ability. The way to get there is to practice. Reconsider sessions outside of the contact with the patient. Eventually, state analysis in the midst of therapy will become effortless.

States may be organized into motivational categories. This includes states that are desired by the person, states the person dreads to enter, and states that result from compromises between such wishes and fears. For example, a person desiring loving attention and fearing rejection may occupy an aloof and muffled state of mind as a defense against the desire to be charming and the threat of then being disregarded.

When a clinician categorizes states into desired, dreaded, and compromises, he or she possesses a motivational view of the patient. That view can be further enhanced by including in the desired state category states that the individual considers as sought-after ideal ones, even though he or she may currently be unable to achieve them. For example, a woman who used a compromise "as-if happy state" wanted but could not achieve a satisfied, authentic state of true intimacy. She labeled the state as "happy face"; it was better then a dreaded state of miserable loneliness.

My research colleagues and I have found it helpful to break down the idea of compromise states into two parts. One is a problematic compromise, as when a person has tense, vigilant, and anxious states to ward off some moods even more dreaded such as monstrous rage. The anxiety symptoms of the tense and apprehensive state may even be seen as the chief complaint at a first interview, hence the general label of "problematic compromise state." With more control another state may be stabilized, for example the kind of aloof mood already used as an illustration. This is then called a "protective compromise" because the mood of remoteness is not regarded as problematic.

The occurrence of each important state, especially problematic compromises and dreaded states, can be discussed with the patient. What events trigger the patient to enter the state described? These instigators of a shift in state may include social events such as changes in the patient's situation; psychological phenomena, such as an emergent memory; or biological

EXHIBIT 2.4
Individualized List of States for Janice

1. Hurt and not working	She appears insulated or aloof, stops tasks, withdraws.
2. Hurt but working	She seems deflated but goes on with her tasks.
3. Tra-la-la	She is cheerful, lighthearted, entertaining, pretending.
4. Crying	She has unrestrained, open weeping. She displays weeping to others to solicit attention.
5. Irritable competitive	She ranges from a covert struggle for a one-up position, to open anger with others, placing blame on others.
6. Acute self-disgust	She is dismayed about some self-realization, with a sense of deflation.

influences such as the effect of drugs or growing fatigue. Important life events may also cause state shifts. A model of state transitions can then lead to a state cycle description. We return to Janice for such an illustration.

CASE EXAMPLE

Janice was depressed with apathetic withdrawal, feelings of fogginess and unreality, and overeating. A label was selected for this state that seemed more individualized than "depressed mood." This label was "hurt and not working," a phrase that she herself used. She could recognize entering and leaving this state.

When in another common state, Janice continued her efforts to work but felt (and appeared) as if her feelings were hurt. This was labeled the "hurt but working" state. There was another state that was different but frequent; it had an external quality of dramatic animation, whereas internally she felt as if she were pretending for the benefit of others. Using her own words for these animated episodes, this was called the "tra-la-la" state. From such beginnings, a list of states was formed that focused on her inner experiences as reported and her manifest behavior as observed (see Exhibit 2.4). As a few sessions passed, states of unrestrained crying, irritability and competitiveness, and acute self-disgust were added to the initial state list.

An example of the closeness of state description to direct material can be seen in excerpts from her therapy. During the second therapy session, Janice had been describing her irritation with her low status at work and how, even in such an undemanding role, her efforts were criticized by her supervisor as inadequate. The therapist commented that she felt degraded at work and then asked if that concept also applied to the therapy situation. This was part of the therapist's effort to understand why she seemed remote from him.

As will be seen, Janice responded by switching between affirmation and disavowal (a habitual style to be discussed in a subsequent step). She did work with the concept, however, and gradually referred to her use of the tra-la-la state to avoid states of feeling and seeming hurt, or even worse, of feeling "acute self-disgust and shame." While describing how she airily told friends she was in therapy, her manner was buoyant and lighthearted. This state prevented her from feeling embarrassed. It became clear that tra-la-la was a protective compromise. It was not what she desired—a more genuine and positive communion—and it was not what she feared—feeling degraded.

Excerpt From the Second Hour of Therapy

T: So, with these kinds of ideas, you're vulnerable to feeling kind of degraded.

P: MmHm [long pause].

T: Well, how about being a patient here? Does that have any current of being degraded?

P: MmHm [pause]. It does and it doesn't. I mean, I've been a lot happier since, since making the decision of actually coming here.

T: MmHm

P: And, like all this past week I went around feeling happy and feeling good. And, you know, a little stronger and stuff. And I knew that it was because I had done something that I hope will be good for me. But at the same time I, yeah, I don't go around telling everybody. Like I'm not going to tell my family; to them my being in therapy would be degrading. They'd say, "What's wrong with you? You shouldn't talk to outsiders. You shouldn't. Oh, you're so weird! You're always so weird!"

And, uh, I make a joke out of it when I tell my friends. That aspect of it, you know, nothing about why and . . . [said lightheartedly, but she trails off and falls silent].

T: That sounds a little like you're *telling them* not to take it seriously.

P: MmHm

T: It's just a lark.

P: MmHm. I'm not allowed to take it seriously.

T: Yeah. [At this point, the clinician observed a momentary transition to a more somber state.]

P: Why am I here? In fact, I almost didn't come today. [This was said more seriously, but then followed by a theatrical enactment of tones of voice used during her tra la-la states.]

I'm, I don't need to come here.

T: Well, you're afraid to take it seriously.

P: Yeah. And, yeah, and all I can say, you know, like I can't say there's something wrong with me. I can't, well, for one thing that's, you know, that's always too dramatic, right? If I sat down and I said, I'm really worried and I'm really unhappy, and, uh, part of me would say [whispers], "Oh, wow, there she goes again. She loves being center stage."

T: Uh, huh.

P: And so I have to say, "Well, it's cause I'm tired of being depressed." And I know there's some things I want to change and I know I can't do it myself. So this is one way of doing it. And that's what I say, if anything, to my friends. I think that's what I said to Phillip. You know, he was really concerned. I just kind of popped in and said, "Oh, guess what I'm going to start doing." And he said, "Eh," and he kind of came back a few minutes later and he was really concerned; "Why are you doing this?"

T: Mm.

P: "I didn't know you were unhappy"—he didn't say that but, you know. . . .

T: Mm. Yeah, *he* took it seriously.

P: MmHm. And so I told him, "Well, you know, I've been depressed. You remember this, you remember that. And I can't do it by myself. So I'm going to do it." And he accepted that [pause]. And, and I mean, I wasn't going to tell him [pause] anything else [pause]. See, I'm not even going to say it *now* [laugh; pause].

T: I'm not going to force you to either.

P: Yeah [pause]. Well, see, I still feel like I'm, *I'm being dramatic.* "What is she keeping undercover? What can't she even admit to herself? [Dramatically and archly said:] Tune in next week."

T: That might be right. You can't expose everything at once.

P: [Laughs] That just goes with the feeling of unreality. I can't even evaluate myself [quiets, and looks serious].

T: Look, you've been checking up on both of us and this situation. And it's a style of yours, to be very private and secret, I think.

P: You know, one of the tools I use to do, that is, to act as if I were being very, very open.

T: Mm.

P: I'm more open than anybody I know, as far as what I'll say about myself, and, and [pause]. . . .

T: Yeah, yeah.

P: And I go around embarrassing people because I tell their secrets, too.

T: Yeah.

P: I've known that, I've just never said it.

Her saying "I'm more open" means the appearance of dramatic, but not deeply felt, spontaneity when in the tra-la-la state.

Excerpts From the Third Hour of Therapy

Other examples of both the hurt but working and the tra-la-la states are found in the third therapy interview. For the first time, Janice described the return home after her brother's hospitalization as a time for reevaluation of the relationship between herself and her parents. Material from later therapy indicated that this episode was extremely important as a recurring memory and topic of concern. But at this early point in therapy she was warding off recognizing its implications. In the excerpt that follows, she gradually entered the dramatic tra-la-la state as she imitated her parents' comments (about how weird she was). Although this shift in state was dramatic and clear on the review of the videotape, where the nonverbal behavior emphasizes the meanings, it is also conveyed in language as transcribed. She begins in a hurt but working state.

T: So the trip back home was also a kind of reevaluation for you and your parents.

P: MmHm.

T: Where they sat you down and had these talks with you.

P: Yeah, and indicated that although they didn't like it [her relationship with Phillip], they had suddenly discovered that they were prejudiced, that they minded very much, they were worried about our rel—, what our relatives would say, they were worried about me, and, you know, potential problems, and all that. I was kind of hurt at some of the stuff they brought up because it sounded like they didn't think I have thought much about it. But, of course, by their view of some of the things I've done, I never think at all. I do all these amazingly stupid things.

T: So, according to their version, I mean, we both know we're carica-
turing it a little bit, you're kind of a nymphomaniac, just running
all over . . .

P: [Interrupts and shifts to the dramatic and lighthearted tra-la-la
state] I'm weird, weird!

T: [Continues] . . . San Francisco and sleeping with everybody.

P: Mm, ahh, Daddy told me I was, I always had been kind of kinky
or something like that.

As she continued on this line, she remained dramatic and in the
pretending tra-la-la state. She used her words for this state in the following
excerpt, where the therapist persisted in trying to get at her own feelings
about herself.

P: Also because I like the idea of the atmosphere and trala-trala-trala.
. . . With them it's a commie-hippie-weirdo college and the only
reason I want to go there is because I'm still reeling. And, and on
and on, and just [pause].

T: I guess you feel undermined.

P: [Whispers really softly] Undermined? [Then resumes a louder vol-
ume] I don't know; I had, I mean I had to get away from them
[her parents]; I can't deal with something when it's real close. One
thing that makes it really hard is that we are very close. I mean,
we're a tight-knit family and I, I really love them [cough]. And so
it's, you know, [she shifts out of the tra-la-la state] it's not as if I
can just push them off and say, ah, whatever. [She trails off into
silence, averting eye contact.]

ADDING SELDOM EXPERIENCED STATES TO THE LIST

Because states are experiential, they can be remembered or fantasized
as well as expressed. Past states as well as possible future states are contemplated, and the desire for or fear of such states can be an influential source
of motivation. That is why a list of states can include those that occur
rarely but have important status in terms of wishes and fears. This is illustrated
for Janice in Table 2.1: It has the six states already listed and adds her most
desired state, an ideal of working authentically in communion with a good,
caring, person. How was she trying to feel when she was in the tra-la-la
state? From what she said in therapy, she wished to feel competent, engaged,
self-confident, happy, frank, and womanly. This again would be a desired
and well-modulated state, one of authentic working, the achievement of
which was an important goal and a motivation for her behavior. Being so

TABLE 2.1
Description of States by Degree of Modulation

Label	Description
Undermodulated states	
Acute self-disgust, shame, or despair (dreaded state)	Feels revulsion at being inappropriate in conduct, fat, and unaccomplished. Most other states are activated to ward off this one.
Hurt and not working	Reads, overeats, refuses social invitations. Feels foggy and unreal; depressed and lonely.
Well-modulated states	
Crying	Displays weeping to others to elicit attention.
Authentic working (desired state)	Competent, authentic, engaged, self-confident, happy, honest, womanly.
Competitive	Critical of or struggles with others to control the situation.
Shimmering state	
Hurt but working	Gives mixed signals, being expressive but with head down while holding, rubbing, or picking self with hands. Displays a leaden face but leaks anxious tension. Talks softly but emotionally, combined with conspicuous self-monitoring and hesitancy.
Overmodulated state	
Tra-la-la	Engaging, perky, histrionic; gestures widen outward, puts attention on other, smiles, makes faces, talks fast, interrupts. Pretends to feel but is quickly distant from the stated ideas. May play act or exaggerate her own ideas and feelings while feeling inwardly at a distance from them. Would like to feel mutually engaged with another or actively creative but feels inwardly at a distance from these ideals as well.

open, however, she might recognize failure or rejection and have so much shame that she would enter a much-dreaded state of self-disgust.

CLOSENESS TO OBSERVATION

Janice would attempt to enter one state while at the same time she was in danger of experiencing another state. She would try to enter the tra-la-la state when she was vulnerable to feeling self-disgusted or hurt. She would try to display this vivacity, but her face might suddenly and quite briefly lose its composure and show a troubled expression. Such acts of will to change states often lead to shimmering states, ones combining a tra-la-la (overmodulated) state (indicated by vocal tone) and a hurt (undermodulated) state (indicated by facial expressions). The discord of signals was apparent to the therapist; he conjectured that it probably also affected her other close relationships.

Transitions Between States

Once states are recognizable, one can ask when they are entered and when they change to other states, this leads to an understanding of how and why state transitions occur and how maladaptive **cycles** can be modified. For example, Janice frequently shifted from the tra-la-la state to the hurt but working state. This shift occurred early in therapy, whenever the therapist actively confronted her with concepts she wished to avoid. If she came too close to expressing these warded-off contents, she was in danger of entering a state of acute self-disgust. On the other hand, whenever she could cope well or successfully institute a defensive maneuver after these confrontations, she exited from the hurt but working state and returned to the tra-la-la state.

Another transition occurred whenever she was abandoned by a person to whom she was attached and had no replacement for this relationship. She then changed from her tra-la-la to her hurt and not working state. Injury to self-esteem could also lead to her hurt and not working state but usually led first to a brief period of acute self-disgust. From the hurt and not working state she might enter the crying state if there was someone else present (see Figure 2.1). In another pattern, one relatively easy to observe, whenever she felt acute self-disgust she quickly entered a competitive state if her interpersonal situation allowed her to blame someone else for shortcomings that were "in the air."

As indicated earlier, the two most frequent states in therapy were tra-la-la and hurt but working. An example of each has been given. The following episode from the first treatment hour illustrates her transition between states.

As part of his exploratory aims, the therapist was about to follow up on a piece of information Janice gave in passing, about living with a male partner (later identified as Phillip). Her first response to his question was within her tra-la-la state, as seen nonverbally by review of videotape and reflected verbally in her words, "Great! Fantastic!" The therapist then made Janice's statement more definite by repeating it firmly. In her response, she indicated a problem she wished to avoid, and then entered the hurt but working state, reflected in the transcript by speech disruptions and on videotape by a lowered vocal tone and facial expression. By the end of the brief excerpt cited next, she said, "I think that's just a prejudice." She left the hurt but working state and was once again in the tra-la-la state.

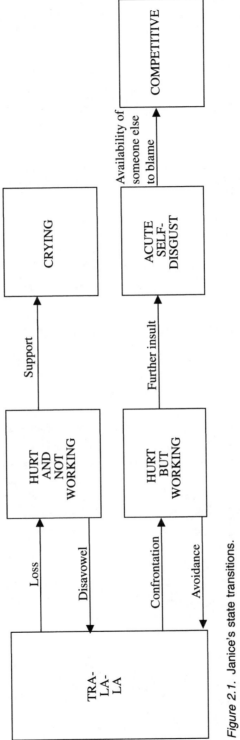

Figure 2.1. Janice's state transitions.

T: Well, you say you have a man-friend. How are things going?

P: Great! Fantastic!

T: That's not blocked then.

P: [Sigh; entry into hurt but working state] There's something there, that [pause] that I don't want to think about.

T: Mm.

P: Um [pause]. Like I, I, one of the reasons I'm afraid of coming here, is I'm afraid that if it helps me get started thinking and growing and kind of heading toward being the person I want to be [pause], I'm afraid it'll mean I have to leave him.

T: MmHm.

P: But I don't know, I, [entry into tra-la-la state] I also think that's just a prejudice I have, and that if I'm not miserable for somebody, or striving to be something I'm not or, you know. [Falls silent.]

State Cycles

As mentioned earlier, from such observations it is possible to model a cycle of states. Such models have explanatory power; they predict that if a person is in a given state and something in particular happens, he or she will then enter another state.

A dreaded state for Janice has already been described, that of acute self-disgust. The desired state—feeling authentically like an active, competent woman in a state of mutuality with another person seldom occurred. The closest she could usually manage to come to this state was the tra-la-la state, which was only superficially like the desired state. She shifted to the hurt but working state when reminded of her shortcomings or conflicts. When these threats to her self-esteem became unbearable she moved back into the tra-la-la state.

Excessive confrontation with her shortcomings in the absence of support from others led to her entry into the acute self-disgust state. She would not remain in that state for long; it was too painful. Instead, she attempted to avoid that state in one of two ways: She would either withdraw immediately and enter the hurt and not working state, or when someone else was available, enter the competitive state and argue that the other person was at fault. This had another advantage: Through competition and challenge, she attracted attention. If she gained sufficient support, as in having an intellectual argument, she could reenter the tra-la-la state. Another exit from the competitive state occurred when she felt too dominant. She then reentered the hurt but working state and felt less powerful. Conversely, when she felt too submissive she tended to shift from the hurt but working state to the competitive state.

State Dynamics

States are the second step of CA, one step beyond the surface observation of phenomena. Yet, even at this close-to-the-surface level, a dynamic formulation is possible. The wish–fear–defense triad is what is meant by the word "dynamic." Taking the patient's stance, the clinician asks, "What states are desired? What states are dreaded? What states serve compromise, defensive or emotional regulatory purposes?"

Usually, overmodulated states are protective compromises: Neither what is desired nor what is dreaded is experienced. Taking as an example the states indicated in Figure 2.1, for Janice the tra-la-la state is a defense against the dreaded acute self-disgust state, with its mortifying degree of felt shame. The inauthentic quality of this state is not what Janice desires, which is true empathic connectivity.

As wishes and fears are clarified into desired and dreaded (or defensive) states, the clinician and patient may become clearer about wish–fear dilemmas. For example, if Janice wanted closeness, her efforts to get closer to a desirable person might risk a humiliating rejection that could catapult her into the feared state of self-disgust. It was safer to avoid this dilemma by keeping a safe distance by role playing, the seeming amiability and affability of the tra-la-la state. Helping patients recognize and deal with their wish–fear dilemmas provides for them valuable insight and a route to better coping skills.

CONCLUSION

States of mind are key concepts in CA; they package together the patient's relevant units of action and experience. Adding states to a formulation system is the key bridge integrating psychodynamic, interpersonal, and cognitive–behavioral approaches. By labeling important recurrent states for the patient, the therapist improves pattern recognition and selective conscious control. Formulation of dreaded and desired or defensive states provides a motivational model. Cycles of states define maladaptive interpersonal sequences. Descriptions of the "whens" of state transition gives vitality to case conceptualizations and write-ups. In addition, technique can be state-oriented; I will consider that topic when I discuss phases of therapy and processes of change.

3

STEP 3: FORMULATING TOPICS OF CONCERN AND DEFENSIVE CONTROL PROCESSES

The third step of configurational analysis (CA) aims to clarify the topics of concern and the defensive control processes that influence how these themes are contemplated.

This step—formulating topics of concern—follows the step of analyzing states of mind quite naturally. The patient may report and the therapist may observe what topics occur with the negative emotions that occur in medleys during undermodulated, shimmering, dreaded, and problematic states. In addition, the therapist observes topics treated avoidantly in over-modulated and compromise states. These important topics are currently active, emotionally arousing, and unresolved because of conflict.

The clinician can begin to clarify excessively pessimistic ways of concluding, as hopeless, a train of thought. The formulation of topics of concern may include statement of dysfunctional cognitions and erroneous beliefs. These may become later targets for corrective efforts using cognitive and dynamic techniques. Some dysfunctional beliefs may be present across several topics of concern, such as "I am incompetent and must depend on others for every decision."

The procedure for formulation in this step can begin by selecting key topics related to phenomena of relevance. For each of these topics, one can consider the central ideas and the degree to which outer reality accords with the patient's conscious views, preconscious attitudes, and unconscious beliefs and assumptions.

The most important inferences are those about discrepancies between realities of the patient's social world and inner intentions, expectations, attitudes, and moral assessments. These discrepancies often evoke emotional responses and lead the person toward the efforts to control emotion that are identified in this step. The formulation includes (a) the unresolved topics; if possible (b) dysfunctional thoughts, ideational discrepancies, or contradictions; (c) typical (but sometimes hidden) emotional response to the discordant ideas; and (d) the defensive control processes used to moderate or halt the emotional response tendencies, which are the potential affects such as rage, despair, terror, shame, and guilt.

One may also examine how much distortion the patient introduces to corrupt rational information processing to accomplish the goal of reducing emotional arousal and so to ward off entry into dreaded states of mind. The more irrational the defensive attitudes expressed, the more danger there exists of the patient entering chaotic, flooded states if the defenses fail or are prematurely pierced in therapy. The techniques used by the therapist to engage topics of concern should be careful, slow, supportive, and tactful (Bond, Gardner, Christian, & Sigal, 1983; Horowitz et al., 1984; Muran, Samstag, Ventur, Segal, & Winston, 2001; Perry & Cooper, 1983; Vaillant, 2002; Westen, 1990).

As with states, the language of problematic topics and the patient's attending avoidance maneuvers is a language that can be shared with the patient. If and when this is desirable, the patient will react positively to the empathy and expertise shown by the therapist. The patient may consequently learn or refine self-observational skills (Horowitz, 2002c). Eventually the patient may even modify defensive character styles, provided a sense of safe readiness to try out new skills of using the mind can be gradually established.

CASE EXAMPLE

Janice's entry complaint was that she was not reacting fully to both the recent diagnosis of her brother's illness and her visit home during his hospitalization. She recognized that to react fully would have been healthy and to not do so was somehow dysfunctional. She was preoccupied with these serious events yet she sensed that her brother's illness and hospitalization led toward trains of thought that she was warding off. These complaints indicated her topics of concern and provided an initial focus for the work of therapy. Other topics were added as the therapy progressed.

Her topics of concern can be divided into three subsidiary sets. One was her reaction to the anticipated loss of her brother, or lack of reaction thereof. A second was her reaction to the visit home, the idea of returning home for good, and a confrontation with the meaning of deciding to continue her life in a city away from home. A third was her reaction to her "silly" behavior around the family when she was at home during her brother's hospitalization.

The anticipated loss of her brother had to result in mourning, in anticipatory grief, at some point. Janice was still in a phase of denial of the reality of the diagnoses possibly leading to the premature end of a relationship. She also avoided implications about her own vulnerability to death or injury; these trains of thought were too frightening. Because of her susceptibility to depression and apathy and her desire to focus on other priorities, she avoided confrontation with such themes. However, she castigated herself for her lack of feeling. She also had to ward off shame and guilt.

The particular therapy period under examination focused not so much on the anticipatory mourning subtheme but rather on the more emergent issues of her dependence–independence theme and on her reaction to her own "silly" behavior during her visit home. That is, therapy started at the surface, not the scariest and most warded-off topics. Therefore, these topics of concern will be used in what follows as primary illustrations. It should be noted, however, that a mourning process of anticipatory grief was initiated during therapy and continued in the posttherapy period.

Janice's brother's hospitalization had led her to return home. When there, her mother requested that now, in view of her brother's illness, Janice should stay home, away from a life that her mother and father both considered improper. To continue work on this dependence–independence theme meant that Janice would have to think through how best to effect her continued autonomy after reentering the nest of her family, how to plan her next career steps and relationships. She warded off ideas of wanting to return home because they contradicted these life aims. Despite such avoidances, however, she remained preoccupied with these issues. This topic tended to return intrusively to awareness with pangs of acute self-disgust, a sure sign that it contained unresolved conflicts.

The reasons for preoccupation with this theme may have had to do with anticipated gains. If Janice could plan for continued development of personal competency and for stabilization of well-being while away from home by developing new skills and more mature attachments to others, then she could hope to become a vibrant woman, one who could feel authentic and self-loving rather than one who felt self-disgust. If she were to remain in limbo, neither dependent nor independent, her depressed states might continue. If she were to return home, then she would never measure up to her own personal ideals, and her self-esteem and interpersonal gratifications would suffer, leading to chronic shame and a sense of hopelessness. She would become too like her mother. One can see that formulation of topics of concern leads to the next step of CA: a fuller inference of key, dysfunctional beliefs and self–other schemas.

The conflict had been unresolved because Janice could not see a way out of her dilemma. If she left her mother, she would have to tolerate feeling bad over hurting her mother's feelings and her anxiety about living alone. She still had some dependent yearnings to regress back to being her mother's own daughter in a familiar home. Independence meant giving up those homesick yearnings, but if she went home, she would have to tolerate her self-disgust at surrendering her aims of being autonomous. Neither path seemed to lead toward good feelings about herself.

Janice used a variety of avoidance techniques to elude the threat of having states of self-disgust as well as experiencing the potential humiliation of communicating self-deflating ideas. She attempted to inhibit the emergence of this topic altogether. If and when this aversion was unsuccessful, Janice used generalization and intellectualization to keep the issue vague, impersonal, and unemotional. When she became emotional in spite of these efforts, she supplemented inhibitory maneuvers by switching attitudes, undoing statements, and reversing roles. When she reversed roles, she externalized threatening traits such as envy or contempt from herself to others. These avoidant maneuvers led to shifts into overmodulated and compromise states, such as the tra-la-la state discussed in the previous step (chap. 2, this volume).

Memories of her behavior during her visit home were difficult to integrate. She felt that, in a social sense, she had not behaved appropriately: She had not cried enough. She contrasted herself with her mother, who cried a great deal. Janice had withdrawn to her room and read instead of participating in family gatherings. Her mother rebuked her for behaving in an inappropriately joking or "silly" manner during this time, as well as for her withdrawal from the group.

Janice tended to remember these moments of silly behavior in therapy because, by thinking them over, she could eventually work through the memories and lay them to rest. For example, she could decide for herself, in retrospect, what behavior had been appropriate and what had been inappropriate. If she felt remorse for her acts, she could forgive herself, apologize, and plan to do better in the future, or perform some other act to express remorse. After thinking through the implications, making up her own mind, planning and executing action, and reorganizing her self and world picture, she could move on to other life tasks.

Before therapy and in early sessions, Janice used defensive controls. These helped her to ward off potential self-rebuke for her immature behavior during her visit home, her yearning to return home to her mother, and her guilt at leaving once again. As already noted, she inhibited the flow of thinking on topics that would be too emotional. She used intellectualization and generalization to avoid direct awareness of her own desire to return home and of her own self-criticism. In communicative contexts, when emotional themes became too threatening, she switched from one attitude to another in her assertion of self-attributes. For example, she might say one phrase that demonstrated her weakness in a situation and follow it with another phrase that demonstrated her strength—one indicated her subordination and the other one indicated her assertiveness. In so doing, she would also exchange roles with the other person. Furthermore, she could externalize attributes, calling her mother selfish when Janice was approaching unwanted conscious ideas about her own selfishness. Having a list of recurrent defensive controls, such as those set in display type, can help the therapist notice and anticipate resistances and obstacles. Counteractive therapist actions can then be planned.

These avoidance maneuvers were not extremely irrational and could be quickly counteracted in therapy if they were not a characterological pattern. But her inhibition, vagueness, disavowal of ideas, and switching between opposite attitudes seemed to be habitual. Change in Janice's habitual patterns was likely to be slow, but her avoidances could still be counteracted by a focus in therapy. These patterns can now be illustrated for the topic that, for the sake of brevity, will be called the "homesickness theme."

EXCERPT FROM THE FIRST THERAPY HOUR

In the first therapy session, emotional inhibition and disavowal were present. For example, Janice gratuitously said, "I don't get homesick," and in the next hour repeated, "Did I tell you I don't get homesick? That I don't miss my family and my friends? Why don't I miss them?" These and several other habitual control maneuvers are illustrated in the following more detailed interchange:

P: She [her girlfriend] misses me a lot.
["She" misses a person, not "I" miss a person; this is a form of externalization of where problems reside.]

And I wonder if it's because the minute she's not there, if I've gotta kind of make her unreal [moving to how "I" feel]—I put her in a timeless slot and I expect her to stay the same, like I can take her out of a drawer. [She does not acknowledge the problem directly, but rather indicates indirectly that she cannot yet accept the realities of permanent separations.]

T: Yes.

P: But it's the same with my family. I don't get homesick. [She disavows inhibited emotions; she does not acknowledge or experience longing.]

T: Yes.

P: I hardly ever get, every once in a while I get homesick. [We infer the underlying thought to be "I hardly ever get homesick." She is correcting "I don't get homesick" but not presenting longing to return home as something problematic.]

In these statements, there is an indication of characterological conflicts and habitual defensive strategies. She struggled between needs for dependence and independence. She wanted to think well of herself but tended to be self-critical. She wanted others to like her, yet criticized them. She wanted to be different from her mother, yet felt a pull to identify with her or yield to her. She wanted to forget her mother's rebukes, but could not put them out of mind.

The need to avoid self-disgust because of the threatening emergence of regressive dependency wishes led to controls that transformed her state. She pretended self-sufficiency and experienced her tra-la-la state. When she thought of herself as competent and on her own, she superficially fulfilled her desire to be independent and mature. She responded to this wish fulfillment by feeling good. Moreover, she wished to stabilize herself in this pleasurable state. Unfortunately, she was unable to do so.

Her behavior was not sufficiently effective to maintain her self-esteem, and she lacked sufficient levels of interpersonal attachments to sustain herself with support. Recognizing these realities made her again think of herself as weak, defective, and needy. A cognitive–behavioral and supportive approach could bolster realistic self-concepts based on increasing competencies and lessening harsh self-criticism. An interpersonal and psychodynamic framework could also increase the complexity of self-awareness, enhance insight, and lead to new decision making.

Another constellation of ideas, emotions, and controls concerns the memory of her behavior at the time her brother was hospitalized, when she conducted herself in a joking manner, did not cry as much as others would think proper, and was accused by her mother of being silly. This theme illustrated her tendency to feel guilt and/or shame. The respondent ideas to this memory were that behaving as she did meant that she was selfish and self-centered. This response conflicted with an attitude that the self should be less important and usually subordinated to the needs of others. Her mother had frequently told her that she felt good about the subordination of her own needs to those of her husband and children. Particularly, at the time of the brother's sudden hospitalization, Janice felt that she ought to care more about what had happened to him than she did about herself, to be selfless rather than selfish.

The comparison of meanings between the idea that she was selfish and the moral injunction to be selfless tended to evoke guilt. She blamed others to avoid a sense of guilt or shame, feelings she believed would be painful and intolerable. She also blamed others when she was vulnerable to enter into states where she would feel ashamed because of the criticism of others.

Janice facilitated the representation of contrasting ideas. One set of ideas revolved around the idea that her mother was bad. That is, she observed that her mother used weeping to get attention. In this way, she could see her mother rather than herself as the one who wanted attention. Another set of contrasting ideas revolved around the idea that she was sad, but her sadness was so strong that she had to bottle it up, and that made her the saddest of all.

Labeling her mother as "the selfish one" seemed to be both true to reality and motivated by defensive aims. This view was supported by a memory of her mother receiving a great deal of sympathy for her worry and anticipatory grief. This view of mother was then related to the attitude, imparted by her mother, that a person should be selfless and care only for others. The incongruence led her to view her mother with contempt and anger. Only a stupid person would subjugate self-interest totally, something her mother also said about herself with self-disgust. Such emotions blunted Janice's tendency to feel ashamed or guilty about her own felt and appraised self-centeredness.

Contempt and anger for her mother was also dangerous. She was vulnerable to feeling anxious or guilty about the degree of rage she could experience toward her mother. This danger could be thwarted by another role reversal: She would again see herself, not her mother, as bad or wrong. She would oscillate back and forth in a continual undoing by either not feeling guilt or not feeling anger about any strong emotional experience. Intellectualization and generalization of ideas helped her to escape further from the threat of these emotions.

When she had gone back to see her brother, her mother had asked her to return to live at home. She had a conflicting response. Her respondent idea was that she wanted to continue her life away from home (to become independent), but she was concerned that this would hurt her mother, who might also see it as Janice being selfish. From the viewpoint of the abiding attitude to not hurt one's mother, her decision to leave again would evoke guilt and shame. To stay home was equally conflicted. Here one glimpses the knotty complexity of a topic of concern. That may be in part why Janice could not resolve this theme on her own. Such complexity may take hours of discussion to become clear.

CONCLUSION

Painful emotions are the reason that conflicted topics are difficult to consider. To prevent entry into an undermodulated state a person finds a way to regulate feelings. One way controls operate is by altering the representation of ideas, feelings, memories, and fantasies. Another way is by altering those self-concepts and role-relationship models that organize trains of thought in various states of mind. This type of defense or coping will be discussed in the next step (see chap. 4, this volume), as various self and other schemas are identified.

4

STEP 4: EXPLORING IDENTITY
AND RELATIONSHIPS

Cognitive–behavioral techniques (CBT) focus on clear formulation of the key errors in thoughts and also clear formulation of more adaptive counter-thoughts about self and others. Interpersonal psychotherapy (IPT) techniques focus on formulation of deficient or maladaptive interpersonal patterns, and also on formulation and encouragement to enact more satisfying and successful patterns. Both IPT and CBT techniques are helped by the psychodynamic formulation of layers of wish–fear–defense.

Psychotherapists using an integrative approach usually aim to modify the patient's dysfunctional beliefs about self in relationship to others and support change away from the maladaptive interpersonal patterns that result. This stage of formulation—of self-concepts and role-relationship models— addresses the schematic basis of such beliefs and behavioral cycles. It deals with the current situation to modify the near future.

Sometimes, as in therapy to modify personality problems, it is useful to extend this step to inferences about how maladaptive attitudes were formed in earlier development. That is, childhood and adolescent situations may be reviewed to clarify how currently inappropriate beliefs and schemas about self and others were formed early and then continued to cast limiting shadows on adult possibilities. Social and biological contributions to roles can also be added to psychological sources. For example, some subcultures advocate for dependent roles and others against them. Some genetic and early social predispositions for leadership (alpha males and females) may exist and tend a person toward controlling others more than average.

The fourth step of configurational analysis (CA) builds on the three preceding steps. For each state of mind one may infer how thinking over topics of concern can be organized by particular self–other expectations, intentions, and roles. That is each topic of concern may be conceptualized, emotionalized, or moderated somewhat differently in different states because the core attitudes, values, and controls vary. In fact, the patient may shift a role-relationship model to change emotionality about a topic of concern, leading to observable shifts in states of mind.

An explanation of relational-emotionality conflicts within unresolved, repetitively contemplated topics is developed in this step of formulation. The method focuses on clarifying the patient's internal models for transactions between self and others. The clinician considers multiple self- and relationship schemas. Some of these **role-relationship models** are more desired and some more dreaded than others. The assumption made is that each state of mind tends to use certain schemas as organizers from a large available repertoire and that by review of narrative, especially stories of and complaints about episodes of interpersonal disappointment, the important elements in this repertoire can be inferred, then clarified and challenged. This confrontation and effort can use varied techniques, examining what works best for the individual patient at a particular phase of therapy.

WORKING WITH THE PATIENT'S IDENTITY
AND RELATIONSHIPS

Recurrent **self-concepts** and interpersonal behavioral patterns can be described in a series of substeps. First, one can make notations as they come to mind about the patient's (a) repertoire of **self- and object schemas**; then see whether one can assemble these gradually into (b) role-relationship models, (c) life agendas and story lines, and (d) repetitive and maladaptive cycles in relationship patterns.

This procedure begins with a disciplined way of listening to or reviewing information from a patient. The discipline involves paying attention to recurrent maladaptive beliefs about identity and relationships. This means listening to both words and music. Eventually, the therapist will help the patient to contrast these beliefs with more adaptive and appropriate alternatives.

This way of listening adds one low-level inference to what is directly expressed by the person. Suppose a patient says when recalling a childhood experience, "What a sneak she was—left alone on a bench where we had lunch, she ate my cookies when I asked her nicely to watch that no one took my lunch." "I wish I had the nerve to scold her but I just ate what

TABLE 4.1
Relationship of Janice's States to Her Self-Concepts

States	Recurrent self-concepts
Tra-la-la	As if an active, competent, creative, and sexual woman, sometimes as if an exceptionally gifted person
Hurt but working	Impaired but learning student
Hurt and not working	Alone, self-sufficient because nothing can be expected from others (warded-off yearning for others)
Crying	Weak, wounded waif; deserving of help, yearning for others
Competitive	Strong, wrongly criticized, inadequately provided for by others
Acute self-disgust, shame, or despair	Defective, fat, lazy, immature, like mother (or "mother's girl") or sexually wrong, greedy, selfish
Ideal	Active, competent, sexual, creative

was left to keep the friendship going." This could be paraphrased as, "I, who am nice, should have scolded her because she was sneaky, but I feared that if I did, she would leave me." Paraphrasing leaves out some contents while amplifying and clarifying self–other concepts.

REPERTOIRE OF SELF- AND OBJECT CONCEPTS

For self-concepts, list the patient's self-concepts that are prominent in each state of mind and then infer the self-view that functions as a major organizing principle for thinking, feeling, and acting when in that state. Each different state does not have to have a different self-concept. It is usually best to start with the most common state. The relationship of Janice's states to her self-concepts is shown in Table 4.1.

For object concepts, list major other-person concepts that seem to serve as predominant organizers in each state of mind. Because roles are occupied by either self or other, some object concepts may be the same as the roles used in the list of self-concepts.

The connection between beliefs is important, and it may be expressed by using words such as "if," "then," "because," "but," "and," and "so." For example, here are some such connections: "My supervisor is critical *and* my father was like that too; *if* I resent my supervisor, *then* he will fire me (and that is the same as my father always threatening to abandon me). I want to talk back and assert my views to my supervisor *but* then he will fire me, *so* I stifle my responses and *then* I get headaches more frequently." These connections lead from dysfunctional beliefs such as "my seniors are always too critical of me" to role-relationship models, such as "I resent seniors for being too critical of me but if I assert my views, they will get rid of me." This look-for-schemas approach to pattern recognition is used in both dynamic and cognitive–behavioral schools of psychotherapy (Curtis et al., 1988; Eells, 1997; Goldfried, 1995; Luborsky & Crits-Christoph, 1990; Norcross & Goldfried, 1992; Persons, 1992; Silberschatz, Curtis, & Nathans, 1989).

For Janice, it was important to note that she expected others to take a superior role and criticize her. Sometimes, however, she reversed the roles and felt superior as she criticized others for their bad habits. The role of superior critic was thus an important one, both for self and others.

ROLE-RELATIONSHIP MODELS

Role-relationship models can be constructed from concepts of the self and others that are repeated and important. As already mentioned, a role-relationship model includes at least four elements: a self-concept or role; the role of the other person; a desire, intention, or feeling toward the other; and an expected action or reaction from the other and the responses of self to these **transactions.** (By the way, remember to refer to the glossary of terms at the end of this book as needed.) These elements may include expressions of emotions, desires, or wishful appetites, as well as threat expectations. A three-person role-relationship model includes additional features, such as envy for the bond between the two others.

Actions can be realistic or quite fantastic: Clinicians may wish to pay attention to magical as well as logical beliefs. The responses and reactions can include critical evaluation and complex emotions such as pride, shame, or guilt. When Janice assumed the role of critical judge of others she was able to find them to blame for disappointments, reducing her own potential to feel shame or guilt. It is wise to not separate thought and emotion, rather to include notations about both.

It is helpful to begin this aspect of case formulation by considering role-relationship models that organize the experience and emotion of the most salient states of mind. For Janice, the most frequent states were tra-la-la and hurt but working. The danger of entering a painful state of acute self-disgust was motivationally important to the oscillation between these states. In this step of formulation, role relationships can be inserted into a model of these state transitions. An example is shown in Figure 4.1.

In the tra-la-la state, Janice tried to feel and behave as if she were an active competent woman in a relationship with another active and competent person. The prototypical transaction was the expression of apparent

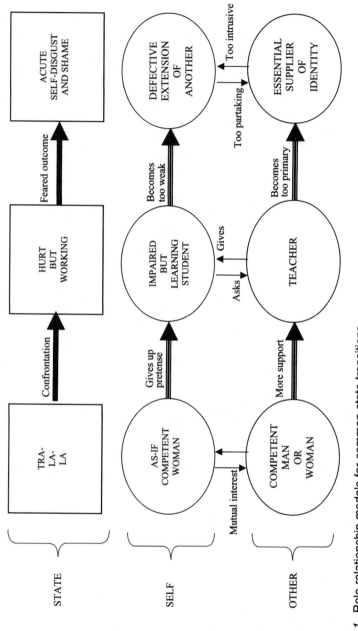

Figure 4.1. Role-relationship models for common state transitions.

mutual interest. In the transition from the tra-la-la to the hurt but working state, she shifted from a schema of self as an as-if woman to a schema of self as an impaired but learning student This enhanced awareness of herself as having difficulties in personal development. She could ask for help and continue to work because she felt she was continuing her personal development in the context of active engagement with a strong teacher or rescuer. She could remain in this state as long as she felt this relationship to be present. If, however, the other was seen as a critical, harsh judge then she would be less hopeful and either more self-disgusted or enraged at the critic (by shifting to the critic role herself and citing anyone criticizing her as grossly unfair and biased).

An example of the transition from the role of the self as if competent to the self as impaired and willing to learn is found in the following excerpt from the beginning of the third therapy session.

EXCERPTS FROM THE THIRD THERAPY HOUR

Janice began in the tra-la-la state, with an animated and humorous imitation of being a patient in psychotherapy with a doctor. The intent of this display was to capture the therapist's interest and perhaps to test his willingness to converse socially rather than to work therapeutically with emotional confrontations about topics of concern. When she was convinced, for the moment, that the therapist was seriously interested in helping her, she shifted to a more serious demeanor and said she had felt depressed. The roles were like a student expressing her impairment and expecting a helpful teacher type of response.

P: [Begins in tra-la-la style] Well, since last time, Doctor, [sniff; dramatic play acting] I find myself storing up things to tell you but, you know, things that happen or things that I think about a lot or something, so, tsk, hm, [play acting] "I'll have to tell him this." [She pauses. The therapist listens quietly and intently. She becomes more nervous as she enters a hurt but working state.] I'm not sure why, whether I think you'll be interested, or whether I think it's relevant. Whether it's something I want to work out. There's something I'd like to work out [pause, continues in hurt but working style]; it happened, has been happening, guess it's still heavy. I got really depressed last week. I don't know what day it started and I couldn't really put a reason to it. No incident, nothing happened. I wasn't thinking any train of thought and suddenly I just got depressed. [Long pause.] It lasted for days and I was just sort of half-functioning at work [a reference to hurt and not working states]; I can't think of a word, I was just oozing my way through the day, and I managed to do a couple of wrong things and [sigh] I'm really upset about that.

The role relationship between impaired learner and teacher was tolerable and somewhat desirable, but it held threats of being criticized and was hard to stabilize. As already discussed, Janice entered it when she gave up the pretense and when support was available.

Janice tended to go beyond the hurt but working state by exaggerating the traits of self and other. Her weaker role of learner, rather than the competent complete woman, could be extended into experiencing herself as too weak in relation to a powerful person. The teacher could be seen as more than a source of ideas or a partial role model and could be seen as now a rescuer, not just a mentor but a principal supplier of Janice's sense of identity. If so, Janice was highly self-critical of her lack of autonomy and vulnerable to her state of self-disgust.

The prototypical situation for developing these roles linked her to her mother. She felt self-disgust and intense shame when she saw herself assuming her mother's identity, becoming a defective extension of her mother rather than a fully independent person. The threat of entering the self-disgust state motivated her to resume the as-if competent self-concept of the tra-la-la state rather than to remain in the hurt but working state. She would make this shift to the tra-la-la state whenever she had made some gain (as in learning something from a teacher) or when she could successfully defend against the "news" about herself that led to the more impaired self-concepts of the hurt but working state.

Obtaining nurturative supplies—even learning from someone—was dangerous in another way (Figure 4.2). Taking from someone could be seen as being too strong as well as too weak: One could take too much and deplete the other. She feared a state in which she would behave like a greedy vampire and suck the other person dry. This concept rested on a primitive belief that psychological supplies such as care are limited and can be exhausted. It could also rest on a covert and dysfunctional family belief grounded in her mother saying, in effect, that she had given so much that if Janice now went away from her, she would feel depleted and misused, as if Janice were a sort of vampire who left her as an emptied person.

Early in therapy, Janice oscillated most of the time between the hurt but working state and the tra-la-la state. She went back into the protective compromise tra-la-la state when (a) she could no longer tolerate awareness that was associated with her concept of self-impairment, (b) she was in danger of seeing herself as taking too much from a rescuing or helping person, and (c) when she successfully avoided contemplating memories that

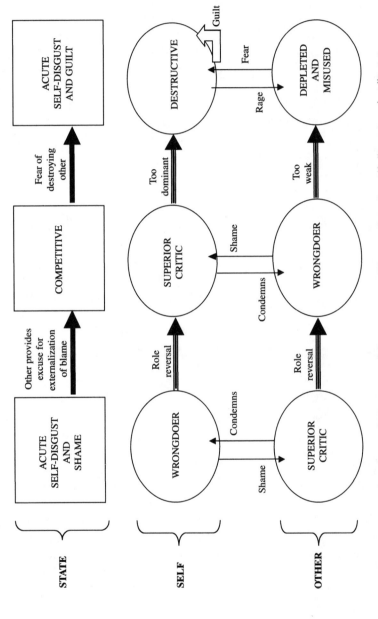

Figure 4.2. Role relationships for the acute self-disgust and shame, competitive, and acute self-disgust and guilt states.

diminished her self-esteem. This was a defensive state shift that was usefully challenged in therapy.

Hurt and Not Working State

The hurt and not working state has already been characterized by an activated self-schema in which Janice needed something but expected nothing and so had to be self-nurturing. This was Janice's state of withdrawal in which the other person was viewed as unworthy, withholding, or lost. There was an illusion of self-sufficiency, as if she were a cocoon and not in need of attachment (Bowlby, 1969; Modell, 1975). If another person became present during this state, Janice shifted from withdrawal into herself as the sole object of her concern to an interest in the other as a potential source of support. This led to a crying state, if such a display of emotion would attract help. There was, however, a feared outcome: She might cry and find no one present or no help offered. This led to a state of acute self-disgust and shame in which she experienced herself as weak, wounded, and in need of a person who would provide total guidance for her but who was unavailable, leaving her helpless. The near certainty of losing her brother as an ally increased her propensity for and fear of this dreaded state.

Janice was vulnerable to self-concepts of being defective or bad in relationship to a superior, critical judge. One example is her having felt that her mother accused her of sexual misdeeds: "I try to justify myself . . . like she's [her mother] sitting up there judging me. And saying, 'You're a slut; you're a nymphomaniac.'" This state, hard for her pride to tolerate, could quickly change. She could shift by projecting bad traits onto another person in a role reversal, illustrated in Figure 4.2. She could then assume the role of superior judge and criticize the other. The competitive state that resulted was a struggle between self and other over who was to blame or who was most defective. This competitive state was unstable because she feared her own destructiveness; her rage might destroy the other.

Configurations of Role-Relationship Models

A **configuration** of role-relationship models can condense many aspects of formulation into quadrants of desired, dreaded, problematic compromise and protective compromise states. Such a configuration for Janice is shown in Figure 4.3. She desired an intimate, mutual connection (her desired intimate sharing state) but feared that closeness will deplete the other (her dreaded acute self-disgust and guilt state); this leaves her in need and without nurture (her problematic compromise: the hurt and not working depressed state). She feels depleted in the hurt, not working, depressed state, her presenting problem. A more protective compromise is the false cheerfulness and limited intimacy of her tra-la-la state.

Patients are motivated in part by aims to avoid dreaded states. These may not occur often and are hard to formulate, but they are important to understand as organized by a dreaded role-relationship model (RRM). Even priming and **preconscious** anticipation of this RRM affects mood and motivates efforts to control emotion. The elements of the RRM lead to clarifications that can be used in whatever techniques that seem most useful for a patient in a given phase of therapy. The RRM information indicates the nature of negative cognitive schemas so important to address in recognizing automatic repetitions of pathogenic beliefs, as in CBT techniques. The RRM information indicates that such obstacles will be serious impediments as the patient attempts to use the positive relationship gambits so strongly encouraged as part of IPT techniques. The RRM information, in relation to desired and defensive RRM, provide the motivational interpretations of personal dilemmas that occur during exploratory psychodynamic techniques. A full understanding helps the therapist integrate all such technical means, choosing the safest and most efficacious route to change.

In some cases, especially the more severe personality disorders, there may be a history of major childhood traumas or repetitive sexual abuse. These severe events may etch dreaded role-relationship models into the personality. It is not the memory of the traumatic events that is alone the problem, but rather it is the embedding of person schemas with extreme roles such as helpless victim and relentless aggressor. In such situations, psychodynamic techniques of exploring how and when role-relationship models developed may be valuable. This linkage of present to past helps reduce dissociations in personal event history and fragmentation in sense of identity. The goal is increasing harmony and reducing chaotic clashes in internalized meanings. If and when such efforts are made, the context has to be one of support, clarity, and endorsement of more adaptive views of how self can articulate with others in the future. Dreaded and desired RRM are often linked associatively: A wish sluices into a fear, creating a dilemma in the way of **character** development. One way to examine knotty dilemmas is to try to fill out a template such as the following: "*If* (I, he, she, they, it) _____, *then* it will follow that (I, he, she, they, it) will _____ (*because*) _____; therefore, _____. For example, one cycle through this map of sequences would be for Janice to give up her identification with her mother—a role of a giving but depleted caretaker—and decide instead to now be a competent, independent career woman with rewarding mutual relationships. A positive sequence is, "*If* I become a skilled person, *then* it will follow that I will get respect because 'they' value competence; therefore, I will work to advance my skills." But there is a dilemma. The positive start can link to a negative consequence.

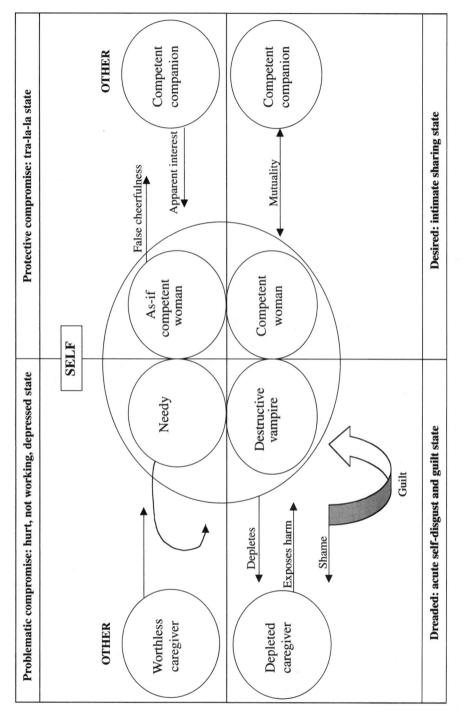

Figure 4.3. A configuration of role-relationship models.

For example, "If I become a skilled person, then it will follow that my mother will feel bad because she will hate being surpassed by her own daughter; therefore to avoid being guilty of that, I will not be ambitious." The appraisal of such diverse beliefs could be a focus in therapy and lead toward awareness, insight, new decision making, and healthier behaviors.

FORMULATION

We can now formulate the case as follows. Janice, in her 20s, still faced the life task of solidifying her own independence and patterns of affiliation to others. She had left home only months before the onset of a serious illness that was likely to kill her brother. His dire hospitalization resulted in a return home by Janice to see him and be with her family. This led to a reactivation of the idea of remaining with her family as expected by her mother. Throughout adolescence, Janice had experienced a strong wish to become a different kind of person from her mother. She chose to act in a manner counter to her mother but as yet felt inauthentic, as if it was an artifice to avoid mimicry of her mother and not a true path for herself. Lack of a sense of hope, purpose, and authentic growth led to demoralization, depression, and helplessness. In a circular way, depressed moods, such as the hurt and not working state, confirmed degraded self-concepts, led to pessimism about the future, and a deepened hopelessness.

Her ambivalent attachment to her mother was connected to her current crisis of how to accept the likelihood of a premature and terrifying loss of her brother and her feeling overwhelmed in planning how to advance and protect her own life.

Many of her statements on the topic of concern of her relationship with her mother expressed ambivalence, not just negativity. The matter was a complex set of wishes, fears, and defenses. For example, she said much later, "When I think now, and I think maybe that's what I wanted, like you reach out, you loop each other's hands, and you look into each other's eyes. And, you know, something has passed between you" [her and her mother]. The other side of her ambivalence was more on the surface, she said early in therapy: "I remember crying one night, a night or so after I came home [after her brother was hospitalized]. Getting really mad at my mother and going upstairs and starting to cry out of anger."

One way to organize such a formulation of ambivalent complexity is what Luborsky (1977, 1984) called a core conflictual relationship theme. A wish leads to various expected but contradictory consequences as follows:

Wish: I want to go ahead and form my own life autonomously from my mother, even though my brother has died and she has asked me to return home, but, these consequences would follow:

1. *Negative response from others*: My mother will be hurt by this separation and I will feel at fault.
2. *Negative response from self*: Because I leave my mother, I will feel frightened and not up to the tasks of working, living alone, and making new attachments.
3. *Positive response from others*: My mother and father and friends will appreciate me for my productivity and successful development.
4. *Positive response from self*: I will feel authentic, useful, and competent so I will feel able to love myself and stop feeling self-disgusted.

Janice had a progressive–regressive dilemma: to live on her own or to return home. The illness of her brother led her to revisit home temporarily and that led her mother to ask her to stop her wanton life away from herself and to return home permanently. This echoed a regressive trend that had been in her own mind: Janice wished she could give up on her push for autonomy, which was lonely and not yet successful; now, in the midst of increased loneliness with the prospect of losing her favorite sibling, she wanted to return home and resume a measure of dependency. If she gave way to this wish, however, her mother might be hurt by her lack of life progression or feel drained in caring for her as a depressed and hopeless person. The mother already had too much to do, Janice believed, in coping with her son's illness, and the mother wanted nurturing for herself. Janice would then feel ashamed for either failing or being engulfed by her mother. She felt guilty for taking sustenance from her mother as if she were a child rather than an adult. On the other hand, her mother would appreciate and love her for returning, and Janice could stop feeling so alone and depressed (were it not for the negative consequences just mentioned).

The formulation coincides with Janice's progressive urge to be on her own but without the depressive consequences of impacted grief and, before that, the difficulties with work and intimate relationships. Therapy would help her aim in this independent direction as a life plan. To get there would require time to work not only on anticipatory mourning for her brother but also on resolving this dependent–independent conflict. In fact, she probably could not work on one without working on the other. The various topics of concern were connected by similar associative appraisals that linked them to the same repertoire of self–other schemas. At the deepest level of formulation one can also consider the degree of integration between schematic configurations. People at discordant levels may require a slower pace of learning in therapy than those at conflicted but less dissociative levels, as discussed elsewhere (Horowitz, 2002b).

CONCLUSION

Formulation is most useful when cases are not simple. Complex cases have multiple states of mind and several interlocking unresolved but highly important emotional topics. Maladaptive cycles through recurrent states may disrupt the chance of sustaining or satisfying interpersonal connections. The repetitive problematic pattern can be clarified by taking the emotions and seeing them as based on social transactional models (Benjamin, 1993). These models are usually person schemas working actively or passively in the mind. These schemas may contain currently dysfunctional attitudes, expectations, and versions of how intentions are implemented and goals approached (or given up).

Everyone has many person schemas that may conflict at conscious and unconscious levels of operation. A useful way when beginning to formulate a case is to list self-concepts, varied by recurrent and important states of mind. Supplementary elaboration will expand and revise this list, while adding relationship concepts. The role-relationship models that emerge can be depicted as models of two persons, three persons, or small group situations.

Modeling key conflicts as role-relationship configurations will then be useful. A quadratic approach to inferring desired, dreaded, problematic, and protective compromise role-relationship models may be helpful, using graphic modes as in Figure 4.3. An integrated formulation can be put together from the analysis of states, topics of concern, and schemas of self and others. Biological, sociological, and developmental factors can be added as needed to the psychological. This formulation forms the basis of treatment planning as well as planning mid-course corrections as therapy proceeds. Many aspects of the formulation, indeed, may be known only in mid-treatment.

II

MID-COURSE CORRECTIONS

5

STEPS 5 AND 6: MODIFYING STATES AND STATE TRANSITIONS AND WORKING THROUGH TOPICS OF CONCERN

Before reviewing the next two steps of configurational analysis (CA), a good question to raise at this point is what obstacles to therapy could we expect on the basis of the formulation derived from Steps 1 through 4?

One likely problem would be how the therapist and Janice could get through her shell of the tra-la-la state and other avoidance behaviors. Some of her obstacles to frank expression could be based on her lack of conviction that she could face and resolve her problems. Remember now that in Step 3 we formulated her as discussing the surface of topics of concern but avoiding their emotional heart by intellectualizing, disavowal, and externalization of blame from self to others. Related obstacles might be Janice's fears of getting too close to a therapist (merging identities, as with her mother), of being criticized, and of her own tendency to reverse roles with a person she expects to criticize her (and so criticizing the way the therapist would do therapy).

Janice was quite defensive, exhibiting prominent overmodulated states and topic avoidances in the initial sessions. But these defenses did not distort reality or excessively project attitudes. The therapist did not expect her to have explosive shifts in emotional state, impulsive acting out, or dissociated experiences of identity and relationship qualities (Horowitz, 2002b). For that reason, the therapy might have been able to proceed relatively rapidly if he could counteract her avoidances and focus on her dilemmas as they occurred in the unresolved topics.

Although Janice had depressive states, the best course seemed to see whether she could make rapid progress without the use of antidepressant medication. The initial focus would be maintained on establishing a **therapeutic alliance** to work together on the meanings to her of her brother's illness and expected death and the familial events surrounding it, especially the request from her mother that she come back home to live. Because of her identity issues, the focus would extend to her decision making about her future choices.

In general, after early sessions, the therapist will have gone from the evaluation level of formulation to a plan of how to stabilize working states by support, how to counteract defensive avoidances by redirection of attention, and how to alter initially conceptualized dysfunctional attitudes and beliefs by interpretation or suggested alternatives. The elements and boundaries of the treatment plan would have been discussed with the patient. In therapy it may be valuable to compare what the therapist suggests with the patient's fantasies of how treatment may work.

To improve formulation, and make mid-course corrections in the direction and techniques of therapy, it is helpful to add phenomena, advance state analysis (Step 5), and see which topics are undergoing new kinds of information processing and emotional expression (Step 6). One also examines relationship processing (Step 7) as discussed in the next chapter. Once again, to aid your review, I set the instructions in display type and subsequently discuss and illustrate them with the case of Janice.

STEP 5: PHENOMENA AND STATES OF MIND: MODIFICATION OF TRANSITIONS BETWEEN STATES

Review changes in phenomena that occur during treatment. What phenomena are new, which have diminished? What states of mind have been modified? What new modes of awareness and expression have occurred? Focus on entry into, and exit from, the problematic states listed in Step 2. In addition, describe the states of the therapist and the therapist and patient as a pair. Describe the effect of therapist interventions on states. Include effects of medication and physical, environmental, social, or situational changes. Discuss with the patient to see if there is a shared view of what is changing and what still needs to change.

STEP 6: MODIFYING CONTROLS AND
WORKING THROUGH TOPICS OF CONCERN

On a key theme identified in Step 3, examine how actions during the therapy affected emotional information processing and defensive efforts to control emotion or resist. What interventions were made by the therapist? How did the patient respond? What, if anything, happened to defensive avoidances or distorting processes such as projection? You may wish to discuss the current focus with the patient and see if it is still a high priority. As a realistic support to hopefulness, clarify improvements. This may improve morale and increase motivation. Review where and when the patient can supply his or her own reinforcement for correction in beliefs and new adaptive behavioral effort.

STEP 5: PHENOMENA AND STATES OF MIND:
MODIFICATION OF THE TRANSITION BETWEEN STATES

As the therapist evaluates progress throughout treatment, the question, "What changes?" is a crucial one. Phenomena, such as symptom changes, are important benchmarks, of course. But as patient and therapist attempt to answer this question, another fruitful place to look is at shifts in the occurrence of states of mind. One hopes to see more well-modulated states.

As in behavior therapy techniques, tracking the course of symptoms, problems in living, and newer, more adaptive actions can be helpful. It indicates where things were, as in the initial list of phenomena, and what has happened. Many patients, now a bit better off, are not yet where they hope to be. They forget initial problem levels. Tracking phenomena indicates to the patient that the therapist remembers such an activity, clarifies progress, improves morale, and focuses additional efforts. As in cognitive therapy, some of the patient's homework can even be directed to increasing awareness of positive changes.

> Toward this end, at times during therapy, the therapist can ask if problematic states occur less frequently. Are dreaded states easier to avert? Are desired states achieved or stabilized? How about states in the crucible of the therapy itself? Do the therapist and patient achieve closer and closer working states with each other? Are overmodulated, avoidant states easier to set aside? Is the therapist having desired states of compassion and empathy?

To observe and describe changes in states, one attends to (a) altered frequency or duration of presenting states, (b) new states, and (c) changes in the conditions that evoke transitions from one state to another. It is then possible to define phases of therapy in terms of shifts in state patterns, as well as how various interventions by the therapist affect the states of the patient. Of course, the many events of the outside world should be included in the analysis of possible causes of change in the patient's states and state cycles.

CASE EXAMPLE

During therapy interviews, Janice most frequently shifted between the tra-la-la and hurt but working states. The competitive-critical, hurt and not working, crying, and acute self-disgust states emerged, but were momentary in duration. The relative frequency of tra-la-la and hurt but working states marked various phases of the treatment: In general, the tra-la-la state occurred less and less, the hurt but working more and more.

In looking at states, one can discern in retrospect that there were five phases of therapy, as delineated by Janice's state patterns.

Phase 1 occupied the first 2 hours. During this time, Janice was mostly in the tra-la-la state; she tested herself in this situation and she tested the therapist to determine the range and variety of his responses, but she remained emotionally remote. No shared focus for the therapy was agreed on.

Phase 2 occupied the third and fourth hours. The hurt and not working state emerged more clearly as both Janice and the therapist began to focus on topics of concern.

Phase 3 occupied the fifth and sixth hours, as well as part of the seventh. There were frequent transitions between the tra-la-la and hurt but working states as Janice tested the therapist to see whether he would force her to maintain this focus.

Phase 4 covered part of the seventh hour and went through the 11th. During this phase, tra-la-la states were less frequent and hurt but working states were more frequent. She worked well on the themes of separation versus dependency, identification, and the existence of bad self-images. She was able to see how these issues related to going home on her brother's deteriorating condition and its aftermath. Janice began to experience sadness about the impending and almost certain loss of her brother during this phase.

Phase 5 was the last hour. Janice was somewhat detached from the therapist and reviewed rather than continued the therapy.

EFFECT OF THERAPIST INTERVENTIONS
ON CHANGES IN STATE

The therapist helped Janice leave the tra-la-la pretending state. When she was warding off conflict in this state, he confronted her by attempting to focus their joint attention on her current problems. This sometimes effected a transition into a working state, in which she examined her shortcomings. Once she was in a working state, he tried to stabilize it by reducing injuries to her self-esteem, and thus prevented transitions to either self-disgust or hurt and not working states. He countered the defenses and evasions that led her back to a tra-la-la state and dealt with her role reversal attempts in an effort to prevent transition to the competitive state.

Janice never became too comfortable in the working state because gradually, as she brought up warded-off content whenever the situation became safe, negative emotions occurred. As therapy progressed, she was able to describe herself as spending less time in the hurt and not working state outside of therapy. Her behavior at work stabilized after the fifth hour and led to a major reduction in the threat of job loss.

Watching videotapes of the therapy, observers noted that the therapist exhibited four states. In one he was inactive but watchful, with rare, momentary, and inhibited facial expressions of frustration or skepticism. This state occurred when Janice remained in the tra-la-la state for an extended period of time. At other times the therapist appeared active, warmly engaging, and hopeful. During such periods, he often offered organized and structured information about difficult choices with which he observed Janice struggling. This state usually occurred when Janice was in the hurt but working state. In his third state, the therapist was verbally inactive but nonverbally empathic. The fourth state of the therapist was less frequent but quite noticeable. His facial expression was earnest; he leaned in toward Janice and made confrontative interventions. This occurred after she had been in the tra-la-la state for some time and would often cause a transition to the hurt but working state. The therapist also would enter this active state when Janice seemed about to shift from hurt but working to the defensive and remote tra-la-la state. The therapist was then often successful in deflecting her from this defensive state transition.

In summary, one of the first parts of describing change in psychotherapy is to identify shifting patterns of state frequency and transition. These patterns may also be analyzed in terms of their relationships to patterns in the therapist's states. Patterns of state changes can be delineated as phases of a change process. The effect of interventions on states, especially as they influence state transitions, is another important aspect of this state analysis. Biological interventions such as medications, and social interventions such as child services, are all important as possible reasons for changes in states. In the illustration case, the most important interventions were psychological support, clarifications, and attention-focusing interpretations.

STEP 6: MODIFYING CONTROLS AND WORKING THROUGH TOPICS OF CONCERN

In Step 6, the topics of concern, dysfunctional beliefs, dreaded emotions, and avoidances of emotion that were formulated earlier are considered in terms of how they are affected by the therapeutic work. This includes a focus on the impact of the therapist's directions, advice, suggestions, interpretations, clarifications, and confrontations. Very often such actions by the therapist focus the patient's attention on aspects of the topics that have been warded off to avert entry into states of mind with too much negative emotion.

Modification of controls facilitates working through the most emotionally conflicted topics of concern. Warded-off emotional responses, once experienced in the safety of therapy, can be desensitized. Dysfunctional beliefs can be counteracted by efforts to repeat corrective concepts and to reappraise what may be reality rather than fantasy. New coping strategies, especially new types of interpersonal transaction or personal skills development, can be planned, tried, revised, and practiced. As new modes become both adaptive and automatic, a modification of habitual forms of control may also occur.

CASE EXAMPLE

Janice came for therapy when she felt depressed. She came in a state of conflict intensified by the illness of her brother and her visit home during his hospitalization. An important topic of concern was the realization that her intended separation from home had not progressed as she had wished. She felt incompetent and overly dependent.

Her wish to be independent and her sense of her own limitations in achieving it were reenacted in several contexts. These reenactments included her actions toward and reactions to her mother during her visit home, her behavioral patterns with supervisors at work, with her boyfriend Phillip, and with the therapist. She felt that she should change jobs and end her relationship with Phillip but that she could not do so because she anticipated job inertia and unendurable loneliness.

At work, she would neither accept direction from a supervisor nor carry out adequate independent work. In therapy, she presented a complaint (lack of emotional response to the impending loss of her brother) that she would not work on when urged to do so by the therapist. She was independent of him in this way but not so independent as to formulate an alternative topic on which to focus the work of therapy.

The therapist repeatedly confronted her about their lack of agreement on the focus of a joint therapeutic effort. Janice then faced the issue more directly after a series of preliminary tests to see whether the therapist would insist on making her submit to dependence on him (in which case she would have to break away) or say she should stop therapy as the mission was unclear (in which case she would be independent but lonely and despondent). With joint effort to avoid either extreme they focused on the homesickness theme.

WORKING THROUGH THE HOMESICKNESS TOPIC

The homesickness topic is a name we can use for the family reunion and the wishes and fears (activated during Janice's visit home) regarding longer standing problems of separation and independence from her mother. Anticipatory grief over the loss of her favorite, most supportive sibling is a part of this topic. During her brother's hospitalization, her mother asked her to remain at home; she had respondent wishes to do so that were incompatible with her stronger wish to become an independent adult. This contrast activated feelings of shame, a state of self-disgust, and a role relationship as a needy child attached to a mother. She inhibited these ideas, disavowed and externalized them onto other persons, and pretended self-sufficiency. Figure 5.1 illustrates the therapist's mid-therapy formulation.

Figure 5.1 puts the sequence of events and states into an explanatory matrix. The ideas, associations, emotional responses, and organizing views of self and others explain the state shifts and the model allows the reader to see the interactions "all at once." In Figure 5.1, the instigating event is the mother saying come home; her inner response is to want to do so, which is associated to failing her ambitions, leading to shame. To avoid shame she has the pretense of acting as if she is self-sufficient, but others do not accept her as calm and productive. The lack of support makes her feel weak, hopeless, and depressed, as shown in more detail on the right side of Figure 5.1. This, once understood, can be contrasted with a change in sequence during therapy, which will be shown in Figure 5.2.

As already described, an indication of her overcontrol and avoidance was found in the first therapy hour when she described a friend who missed her a lot, whom she herself did not miss. She added, "But it's the same with my family; I don't get homesick." When the therapist agreed with this, she hinted that it was not really the case by adding, "I hardly ever get, every once in a while I get homesick." This same disavowal and role reversal was present again in the second therapy hour when she said, "Did I tell you that I never get homesick? That I don't miss my family and I don't miss my friends?"

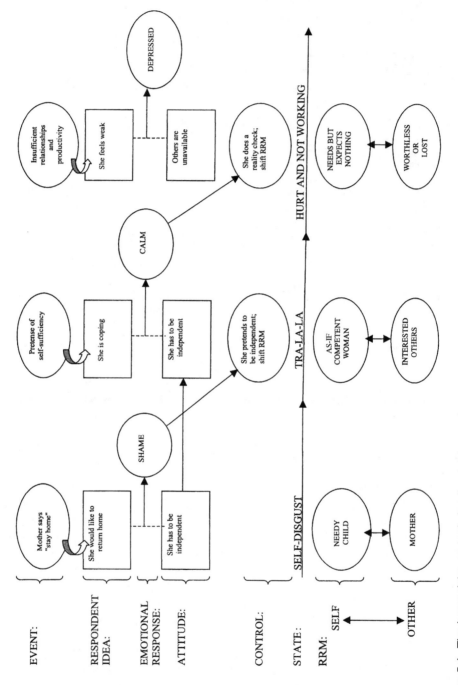

Figure 5.1. The homesickness topic leading to depression.

As a contrast, later in therapy she could acknowledge homesickness while maintaining her desire for independence. For example, in the 10th therapy hour she described how, on arriving home after her brother had been hospitalized, "I came off the plane with a lip-trembling kind of thing and, at various times, I could have fallen on her [her mother's] breast with tears and wailed." In the 11th therapy hour, she was able to say, "When I think about it now, I think maybe that's what I wanted, you know, like you reach out and you loop each other's hands and you look into each other's eyes, and then you know something has passed between you."

Janice's acceptance of a working focus on this theme was aided by establishing a sense of empathy in the therapeutic relationship. The homesickness topic was transformed into a cycle that led toward a hopeful conclusion, as shown in Figure 5.2. This process, enhanced by the therapist's actions, will now be illustrated in detail.

EFFECT OF THERAPIST ON CONTROLS

On her own, early in therapy, Janice could not stabilize a self-image as a student learning how to become independent because she tended to be overly self-critical. She was threatened by the strength of her wish to return home and the associated self-image as a needy child searching for a rescuer. For these reasons, she inhibited such ideas and facilitated counter ideas of self-sufficiency. These controls impeded a planned approach to confronting and resolving her problems. By focusing attention on the theme, the therapist counteracted her avoidance strategy.

Developing and stabilizing a sense of compassion from the therapist increased Janice's tolerance for her own negative emotional responses, such as shame. The therapist's interventions gradually challenged her defenses and then helped her to process warded-off ideas. In other words, with an emphasis on the alliance of the therapeutic relationship, the therapist could hold her to the homesickness versus independence theme by using support plus sequential repetition, clarification, and interpretation. With her increased anxiety tolerance, Janice could now pay attention to her conflict and plan on how to further her development. As she developed usable plans, she felt increased hope and so could tolerate additional facets of a working-through process. In contrast to the inhibition of ideas and pretense of self-sufficiency shown in Figure 5.1, the effects of the relationship permitted the flow of ideas and emotional expressiveness shown in Figure 5.2.

The therapist aimed to counteract Janice's inhibition of expression of key topics. Then, gradually, the therapist dealt with her switching between counter themes within a topical focus. Next he challenged her disavowal of the importance of central emotional ideas in each subtopic.

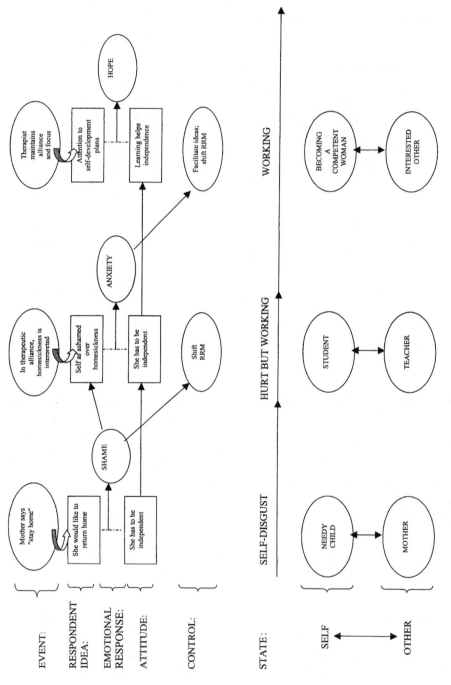

Figure 5.2. The homesickness topic leading to hope.

MODIFICATION OF INHIBITION

The therapist attempted to find words with which to label warded-off ideas and feelings. An example of this type of work is found in the fifth therapy hour. The therapist had used the word "lonely." Janice disagreed with the term but expressed a semblance of agreement about the feeling. He sided slightly with her disagreement but continued to confront her with the word. Finally, he made a direct interpretation, saying that he thought she was homesick. She admitted it for the first time; she then shifted from the working state to the tra-la-la state and said it was not people for whom she was homesick but her own childhood.

P: Un-huh. Why would a [long pause]. It seems funny to say, lonely. I can't quite agree, but I can't disagree [pause]. In some ways, I had a really, really happy childhood.

T: Yeah. That's why it seems funny that I find myself using that word, yet you come across to me as being lonely.

P: Hm [pause].

T: I have a feeling that you're homesick.

P: Do you remember that hot weather? [Pause.] Um, what was it a week and a half ago?

T: Yeah.

P: I got so homesick and that's the first time, really, since being out here. I've had one or two flashes. Once when it rained I thought of our house by the lake. I wanted to be there. But that hot weather [pause], in the summer its really hot and muggy, and [pause] I was really homesick, and it wasn't for the people, as they are now, it was for my childhood. I wanted to be at the lake. I wanted to go hiking with my brothers [pause]. You know, to fish [pause], sit in the living room and listen to the rocking chair creak, and somebody making tea, and everything!

T: Uh-huh. Well, it sounds nice.

P: Oh, it's really [pause] that's [pause] that's my home, by the lake.

DEALING WITH SWITCHING MANEUVERS

Another control that Janice used to deflect from processing ideas in this constellation involved switching back and forth between various attitudes. The therapist reacted to this with efforts to hold her to a specific attitude by imposing pointed questions or repeating phrases. Finally, he developed a specific nuance of technique, reinforced by Janice, who would then present her thoughts more openly. He would repeatedly verbalize her disavowal, "I see that you are not at all homesick." This prompted Janice to state the opposite position more clearly and firmly, as if asserting her independence from the therapist's position. In doing so, she often said more than she would have said had the therapist not verbalized the disavowal as if it were his position.

An example is the following excerpt from the seventh hour. The therapist asked her to consciously intellectualize, to deliberately use a manner of control she ordinarily used unconsciously.

> T: But let's be, let's be very rational, very intellectual about it. What does it really mean to you that Sam [her brother] is seriously ill? In terms of you, what does it mean?
>
> P: My life?
>
> T: What meanings does it have? Be very reasonable.
>
> P: Well, nothing in terms of the things like coming in and giving hugs and stuff. It means that occasional letter that isn't there because he is too sick to write, the admiration that he had for me. That asking for big sisterly advice kind of thing [long pause]. It means I don't like the mention of illness now. Um, it doesn't mean anything that I can put my finger on.
>
> T: Yeah. You know, we just look at that level, and it doesn't have any big implications for your life on that level at all.

The therapist made his assertion at the disavowal position in her oscillation between "it does" and "it doesn't" have meanings. She then asserted the reverse of his statement more distinctly.

> P: In a way it does, because it really brings home the reality of things. And, like, he was there, healthy and functioning. I hadn't seen him for a year, but I knew he was there. I had the faith; I believed he was there. And now he's not there in the same way, and I have to take that on faith too [sniffles]. I'm so, uh, what's real and what isn't? Is anybody real? Now, all these people that I remember, that I feel close to, that I have this faith in. Maybe they're not real either.
>
> T: Well, it symbolizes, then, a larger realm of meanings, which is that the family that you were attached to, your childhood and adolescent family, is no longer there for you. Because you're no longer a child or an adolescent. You've become independent.

Note that the therapist has again taken a position by saying that she has already become independent. He is saying, in effect, that she is not homesick. She can oppose him by saying that she gets homesick. She does this by saying, "When I get homesick," in what followed immediately after the above remark:

P: When I get homesick, I get homesick for childhood things and places. It's not a present-day kind of homesickness. It's not like I physically want to go back there and do what's going on now, or I'd live there now. I want to go back in time, too [long pause].

T: Sure. Then you had some pretty reliable ties with people. Your ties to Phillip [her current boyfriend] aren't so reliable [pause].

P: No, not at all.

COUNTERACTING DISAVOWAL

At this phase of therapy, Janice still maintained her distance from the homesickness topic by failing to connect it with her needy child self-images; she used her competent self-images instead. In other words, she expressed the theme with objectivity rather than subjectivity, in the tra-la-la state rather than in a working state. The therapist's next task was to counteract this disavowal of emotion.

Here is an example from the ninth hour of how the therapist confronted Janice with her distancing of herself from a real encounter with herself:

T: I have a feeling you're moving away from me. I don't really have a clear picture and I feel you're not making what you want to do clear to me.

In a way, the therapist took her position. He was not clearly understanding her, just as she was not directly experiencing the theme. He repeated this challenge, asking that she make him understand. Because a therapeutic alliance had been established before this middle phase of therapy, he was able to be incisive. She shared his confidence in her ability to confront the warded-off ideas and feelings. Even in a struggle with him, she could maintain a "strong" self-image to counteract the danger of emergence of her weak, dejected, and "disgusting" self-image. The excerpt continues with an example of such ongoing efforts at confrontation.

P: Well, it's 'cause it's not clear to me. You see, because I'm not thinking about what is this for, where am I going uh, what I'm doing is not working.

T: [Incisively] You're not working and you're not going to get married to Phillip and that's about where you're at. And. . . .

P: [More argumentative] I'm waiting [pause] I'm waiting for Bob and Carol [friends from home] to come out.

T: Yeah, and they're bringing a fortune cookie with the answer to it in there?

This was unnecessary sarcasm and could have damaged the relationship. It is a countertransference sign of the therapist's impatience. However, the alliance was such that the patient understood the remark as humor to perforate her rationalization for procrastinating.

P: [Subdued, earnest, reflective] Maybe. Yeah. They're bringing me [pause]. They're bringing [pause] a [pause] me [pause] that I like. They both love me.

T: Um-hm

P: And they let me know it!

P: And they've known me for about ten years or more [pause]. And I'm counting on having their support and having them to bounce myself off of.

T: [Incisively] Yeah, but what about me? Why? Why am I in the dark now? Why am I feeling that I don't know what's going on with you?

P: I don't know. I don't feel that I'm trying to hide anything from you particularly.
    It's probably just 'cause I, I don't [she trails off].

T: [Earnestly] I thought maybe you were sharing that feeling, though.

P: Like what? That I don't know what's going on?

T: Yeah.

P: [Somewhat petulantly] Well, I just don't want to think about it. I don't want to think, "Where am I going?" or "What am I doing?"

T: [Firmly] Yeah, but what would you think of me if I let you get away with that?

This is an example of the therapist taking on her role; were he to let her get away with it, he would be the lazy one who allowed her life to stagnate. He is trying to help her to contemplate "laziness" by taking the role on himself and asking her to react to him as lazy about understanding her.

P: No, I mean that's probably why you feel hazy is because I'm being purposely hazy to myself.

T: [Firmly] Yeah, but what will you think of me if I don't say anything about that, if I just let it just roll on like that?

P: You're probably as fuzzy as I am.

T: We have a limited amount of time. What if I didn't say anything and just kept silent? I mean it. What would you think of me?

P: [Pause] I'm not say—[pause].

T: Would it be okay with you if I would not say anything else about that?

P: I might not even notice, probably, underneath. But, see, I'm not even sure what [pause], what it is that you're keeping silent about. And I [pause], I'm getting very confused, too.

T: MmHm. Oh.

P: [Very vague] Uhm, if you didn't think anything about your confusion, about where I am and what I'm doing right now [she trails off].

T: Not thinking would be a version of what we're calling laziness.

P: I don't know if that's what I am doing. It's fear and laziness. I don't want to think. I want to kick the whole thing off. I don't want to do much more than what I'm doing with you. I don't want to think about, un [pause, then incisively] going to school. I don't want to think about the fall. Do I really want that job back again? If not, what else? I don't want to think about the kind of person that I want to be.

The patient was being firm now, like the therapist and may have expected the therapist to sit back because she had been a good student, saying something the teacher wanted to hear. But the therapist decided to press on by having her contemplate how she would react to his taking the "lazy" position.

T: Yeah, but the question says, "What will you think of me if I go on with that position?" I'll say, "I don't want to deal with her."

P: [Interrupts] I've got [pause] I mean [pause]—

T: [Overriding her] "I don't want to deal with her. I don't want to deal with her in that way."

P: [Becomes petulant] Um, I'd probably stop coming [pause]. If that was your attitude, I mean, if it came through to me that way, that you didn't press certain issues because "Well, we only have so much time and, after all, we can stick to the easy ones." Cause, uhm, that would make me feel [pause] rejected, and uhm, uninteresting, unimportant.

Repeated confrontation does not, with Janice, lead to some dramatic end point of either revelation or decision. That is not her style. It does, however, increase her time spent focusing on the topic during the therapy hour. More important, it increases her time spent focusing on the topic outside of the interview, because it is her style to work over in her mind at other times the incomplete, emphasized, or troublesome interchanges that occurred during therapy.

CONCLUSION

This sixth step of CA concerns how topics of concern are worked through (or not). It includes consideration of how these topics relate to states and organized views about identity and relationships, as formulated in earlier steps. The effects of actions by the therapist are considered.

A key aspect of a therapist intervention is that they affect the focus of the patient's attention. This affects the patient's habitual efforts to control emotions and ideas. The general goal is to increase conscious contemplation as a skill to facilitate a clearer, deeper, and more continuous focus of attention. This awareness-enhancement process occurs in the midst of the panoply of relationships discussed in the next chapter and is reinforced by realistic, positive, and hopeful attitudes toward the therapy by both patient and therapist. It is also increased by insight and new discussions about what to express and examine in the company of the therapist and significant others.

6

STEP 7: WORKING ON VIEWS OF SELF AND RELATIONSHIPS

Analyze the roles of patient and therapist with regard to alliances and other relationship patterns such as those of **transference** and counter-transference. Clarify the effects of separations and new attachments. Indicate relationship dilemmas of the therapist, such as facing a patient who will become dependent if directions are offered or become disorganized if the therapist offers no guidance on decision making. Describe new relationships or beliefs and the patient's psychological mindedness and changes in ability at self-appraisals and stance in self-criticism. Discuss key role-relationship configurations with the patient and see where there is agreement and disagreement on what each party experiences and now expects about the other. Are obstacles to full and frank discussions becoming less frequent as the role relationship model for a therapeutic alliance is enhanced?

This is a good place to summarize sessions 5 through 9, because the issue of self and relationships, including Janice's relationship with the therapist, were focused most intensely in these sessions.

Janice seemed more open to communicative give and take in the fifth session. The hour focused on the issue of establishing a therapeutic focus. She had become diffuse and remained emotionally avoidant when asked what she wanted. She replied that she wanted the therapist to somehow give her "an acceptable image of herself." He said that would be difficult because she did not want to express her feelings of herself as in some other way "unacceptable." There was some additional work on recognizing a passive–aggressive pattern in terms of how this transactional style had provoked criticism from her supervisor at work.

In the sixth session, she talked about Phillip and how she would like to get away from him if she could only bear the thought of being alone. She tested the therapist to see how much he would offer to do for her; she wavered between disclosing more of herself and trying to present a superficially good picture. The therapist listened during most of the hour and made an occasional intervention to link her difficulties with Phillip to her degraded self-images. In his process notes, he remarked that he felt they were unfocused without much work being accomplished.

In the seventh session, Janice asked the therapist to state his goals of therapy. He discussed aspects of his formulation with her, including topics of concern and several relationship themes, and also his own uncertainty regarding a joint focus. Was her brother's illness the most important topic? As a result of this discussion, an increasing sense of clarity and trust seemed to strengthen the working relationship. She then reported a dream about her brother; she had had the dream the night before this session. In the dream, he told her not to worry about him because he was fighting his illness and even if he lost the fight, she still had other siblings.

In the eighth session, Janice indicated that she had had turbulent feelings since the previous interview. That including crying for a whole day, but she felt better as the present interview approached. She indicated improvement in her ability to avoid both excessive eating and withdrawing from others. She talked of how she cried or used a story about losing her brother to get sympathy. The therapist then centered on how she had left her family, was uncommitted to a future plan, and so felt homesick.

The patient and therapist then discussed how her brother's hospitalization had intensified her wish to return home. She had always felt a pull to be like her mother and yet had an even stronger wish to separate herself from her mother and seek out her own roles. With clarity on this conflict, and equidistance of the therapist from either choice she might make in the midst of this conflict of dueling wishes and dueling values, Janice then showed a much greater feeling of cooperation and alliance with the therapist. Therapeutic interventions linked her frustrated search for a secure attachment with her reactive feelings of contempt and hostility toward those with whom she did not connect.

In the ninth session, Janice came prepared to talk about her perceived bad images of herself in relation to Phillip, her domestic partner. The therapist listened for a long time and then confronted her with her vagueness and distance from him (the therapist). The hour then focused on her difficulties in adjusting after leaving her family; it also focused on the relationship of the visit home during her brother's hospitalization to her struggle over whether to return to or escape from the influence of her parents.

ROLE-RELATIONSHIP MODELS

The patient and the therapist each bring their individual scripts and schemas for their selves and their relationships to therapy. As they interact, they gradually develop new ways of relating. This can lead to the development of new, more adaptive role-relationship models in the patient. In addition, the patient learns by identifying with the adaptive ways of the therapist. Also, as the patient gains insight and control, he or she engages in and learns from new forms of social interaction outside of therapy. Thus, new role-relationship models are learned from experiences with the therapist, both "in role" and by identification, and from trial and practice of new actions in other relationships.

The therapeutic relationship is the most thoroughly studied aspect of psychotherapy (Alexander & French, 1946; Frank, 1974; Freud, 1912/1955; Gill, 1982; Gill & Hoffman, 1982; Greenson, 1967; Kohut, 1978; Langs, 1976; Loewald, 1960; Luborsky, 1984; Wallerstein, 1986). Many have emphasized the special importance to change of a new emotional–relational experience with the therapist. This opportunity for modification of relational expectations and intentionalities is enhanced when the patient and the therapist can consciously review simultaneous alternatives (Horowitz, 1998; Horowitz, Kernberg, et al., 1993). They contemplate and compare roles occupied during maladaptive interpersonal patterns with roles of more adaptive attitudes. These moments can be pivotal: Primitive schemas can be revised and new levels of mutuality achieved.

Adaptive and maladaptive inner models of a relationship can be contrasted in one or all of three time frames: the past, the present, and the imagined future. The present can be examined in stories of relationships outside the therapy situation and in the direct observation of the therapy. The therapy is examined by observing both verbal and nonverbal communications and paraphrasing significant self–other patterns. The most difficult task for beginning therapists is to examine those patterns that may occur in the nonverbal behaviors—that is, in the music of the therapy situation.

In addition to learning new role-relationship models, a patient may also advance by integrating existing role-relationship models into **supraordinate schemas.** The patient may thus soften ambivalence, realizing that they may both love and hate in an intense affiliation rather than dissociating the attitudes toward the other into all-good or all-bad states. Basic elements of the patient's character remain the same, perhaps, but they are harmonized.

In CA of change in person schemas, it is sometimes helpful to begin with obstacles to therapy or reenactment in therapy of maladaptive patterns. This can be done by inferring role-relationships of transference and counter-transference problems. One aims toward contrasting these role-relationship models with the optimal relationship potentials and also with improved and realistic therapeutic alliances achieved by patient and therapist. This optimal adaptive relationship of the therapeutic alliance can provide a point of reference to better describe relational patterns that deflect from it. These will include attempts by the patient that fall short of a therapeutic alliance, as when the patient manifests a transference or, in a protective compromise state, tries to set up a social situation instead of a therapeutic engagement.

> Fluctuations in current and past views of vital relationships should be described and explained in this step of analyzing process from a relational point of view. This includes reasons for the major entries, exits, and changes that involve figures other than the therapist. Similarly, the therapist should examine the process of revising attitudes about past affiliations (e.g., the replacement of childhood views of parents with current adult appraisals). New views of future possibilities for relationships are also important components at this level of analysis.

THERAPEUTIC ALLIANCE

An initial therapeutic alliance is itself a kind of transference because it partakes of a role-relationship model already available to the patient. This role-relationship model may use the patient's most trusting and advanced **person schemas.** Two other types of relationships offered by the patient often fall short of a therapeutic alliance. One tendency, already mentioned, involves the patient seeking a social relationship with the therapist. Instead of an encounter with his difficulties, the patient tries to present a facade of normality by, for example, bantering with the therapist. The second tendency involves the patient seeking a direct need-fulfilling relationship with the therapist, one in which the therapist would give ideal love, absolution, total care, or restoration of lost ties to another person. There are, of course, other tendencies as well, such as those expectations of failure, exploitation, or incompetence that lead to negative transferences and countertransferences.

Most patients test or provoke the therapist to see whether dreaded or desired role-relationship models will apply to this situation. He or she examines the therapist's verbal and nonverbal actions to see whether social interchange will be enough, to see whether the match is stable enough to warrant a therapeutic alliance, and to see whether transference gratifications or threats might be possible (Langs, 1976; Weiss, 1993; Weiss, Sampson,

& the Mount Zion Psychotherapy Research Group, 1986). These tests are meant to determine not only what wishes might be gratified but also what fears are warranted. In general, the patient wants to see whether the therapist will hold steady on developing a therapeutic alliance rather than engaging in social conversation or transference–countertransference roles of relationship.

Although the initial therapeutic alliance is based on existing role-relationship models, later therapeutic alliances may modify this base to accord with the realistic qualities found in the transactions of therapy. Some patients learn the basis of increasing trust, interdependent work, and a sense of cooperation for the first time.

In the middle of therapy, if a therapeutic alliance has been developed, many patients reverse roles; they thrust the therapist in the very role that has been difficult for them—the patients—to manage. For example, a patient who has been unable to cope well with insatiable demands from a critical other may make many demands on the therapist and then complain that the requests are not fulfilled. The therapist's coping operations and ability to handle the dilemma of giving too much or too little is then copied by the patient. This process of learning by identification usually occurs outside of the clear, self-reflective awareness of both parties. CA involves examining such relationship patterns inside of therapy and searching for links to repetitive relationship patterns in general to identify the processes of change that may affect patterns in other relationships.

Understanding the shifting states of social alliances, therapeutic alliances, and transference–countertransference alliances has been the particular province of psychodynamic schools of thought. Occupation by the therapist of a role as an expert leader in cognitive–behavioral therapy techniques reduces patient role ambiguity, provides many patients with a sense of clarity in direction and hopefulness. Even so, transferences will perhaps occur but they will usually be passed over unless obstructive. In interpersonal therapies the transferential patterns are also not focused on; the goal is to modify outside-of-therapy relationship patterns. Whatever the technical approach used, however, it is widely accepted that advantages are gained for the patient when the therapists can recognize and formulate transference and countertransference patterns and decide how to use the information. The therapist will then use an integrative approach, perhaps choosing which techniques to use when, allowing him or her at times to interpret the transference phenomena if and when this is (a) needed for change, (b) needed to reduce obstacles, and (c) not likely to further disorganize the thinking of his or her patient. Recognizing transference does not necessarily mean interpreting it to the patient, and if it is interpreted the therapist may chose whether to focus on the pattern in the therapy, in current outside relationships or in relationship stories of the past.

CASE EXAMPLE

The Therapeutic Alliance Model

As noted earlier, each individual has a repertoire of self–other schemas. For Janice, the therapeutic alliance corresponded most closely to the role relationship in which she was learning and needing to learn and in which the other (the therapist) was assigned a role (in her inner **working model**) of a teacher strong enough to help her. While working on a foundation for the therapeutic alliance, she viewed herself as a person "en route" to maturation into adulthood although at present impaired by immature attributes. Moreover, she believed the therapist viewed her that way. Reciprocally, she read into the therapist and assumed that the therapist viewed himself as a calm, hopeful, interested teacher. Furthermore, she believed that the therapist believed that she viewed him that way.

In a state of mind organized by this sense of alliance, Janice was able to see herself as providing information about her impairments. In a complementary fashion, she saw the therapist as seeking that information by helping to increase her awareness, by clarifying and by constructing meaning through interpretation. She saw him as a teacher who might comment on her weaknesses to help her gain strength. He worked on her behalf, but he also stood for fidelity to reality. She could identify with his stance and join in it; she too was seeking information about her impairments and knowledge of how to change.

In states during therapy within this safe alliance, the therapist was able to see through her pretenses, tactfully point out lapses from Janice taking the role of a learning student. It was important for Janice to see herself as a person in control of the learning process, and one not overwhelmed by recognizing her underdevelopment. Both felt that she was able to face the tasks of self-confrontation in therapy and accept responsibility for new decisions.

As indicated in the previous section, this alliance developed slowly over the first 6 hours, but was well-established by the end of hour 7, allowing the working through of important conceptual constellations during the remaining therapy hours.

The Social Relationship Model

During the first half of the therapy, the threat of the emergence of dreaded states of self-disgust with shame or guilt was avoided by her tra-la-la state with its self-concepts of an as-if competent woman. The relevant figure is reproduced here as Figure 6.1. As indicated in the figure, Janice resisted a therapeutic alliance by offering instead a social relationship in

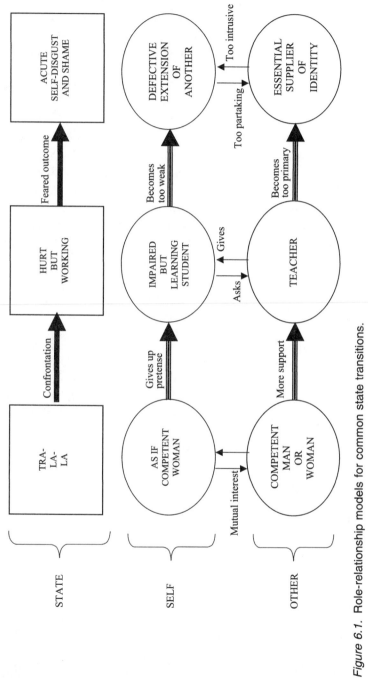

Figure 6.1. Role-relationship models for common state transitions.

which intellectual or bantering conversation would dominate. For her, this occurred in her tra-la-la state.

Efforts by the therapist to confront important topics caused a transition from the tra-la-la to the hurt but working state. The confrontations led from the self-presentation as-if fully competent to a presentation of self as having areas of limitation. As she entered the student–teacher role-relationship model she used for the therapeutic alliance, she found the role of being "a learner of adult life" more acceptable. As this role became easier, there was less potential for hurt and shame, and so less need to escape from the working state back into the tra-la-la state with its as-if competent self-images.

As we have seen, one tendency to misalliance was to present herself as being too well—as being already a competent woman—and to set up a social relationship as a cordial intellectual companion to the therapist. This was, after all, the stance she took with friends and at work. These as-if competent self-presentations also functioned as tests to see whether the therapist could be taken in or whether he would insist on authentic work. It was a misalliance because the pretense was destructive; seeing herself as being already totally competent was a habitual compensatory strategy that interfered with her potential work of therapy.

The Transferences Model

There was another tendency to misalliance based on antithetical behavior. In that misalliance, Janice saw herself as doing poorly and as if the therapist had to rescue her completely. Gambits toward such a misalliance were apparent early; there were repeated requests that the therapist give her blanket reassurances, that he dispel her depressions, and that he buffer her difficulties at work by giving her written excuses. These gambits occurred in the first five therapy sessions, were noted by the therapist, and were responded to in a way that strengthened the therapeutic alliance but avoided criticism of her.

If the therapist were to agree to be a total rescuer, Janice would have found in him an ideal parent. This type of needy and weak self-image in relation to a totally rescuing parent was expressed late in therapy in this way: "I wish I could get sick and be in the hospital, or go crazy and be in a mental hospital, or, you know, not having to be responsible." It was important to this patient that the therapist not accept such dependency and that he side with her aims for competent independence.

On the other hand, when the therapist refused to provide supplies and rescue, Janice tended to feel frustrated, criticized, and defective. She then turned the tables and criticized him as a too-orthodox therapist, a male who could not understand a woman. She challenged his confrontations as off-target. He was the one who could not agree on a topic for a joint focus early in therapy.

In a repeated-state transition pattern noted in Figure 6.2, Janice saw the therapist as a superior critic in relation to herself as defective. In this self-disgust state, his role corresponded to a role her mother sometimes held when criticizing her for being promiscuous or a role held by her father, who accused her of laziness. Such dangers led her to avoid expected criticisms by not discussing her troubled relationship with Phillip, her difficulties in working, or her reasons for coming into treatment. The therapist, she thought, would only humiliate her if she discussed these topics. As a defense, she reversed roles and criticized him. But the resulting state of competition or temper outburst was a threat. She could therefore feel disgusted with herself for apparently demolishing her image of him. This is linked to a dysfunctional belief that her successful independence would humiliate and demolish her ineffective mother.

Other elements of the therapy situation contributed to difficulties in establishing a therapeutic alliance. She gave consent to videotaping for teaching and research purposes. These factors limited confidentiality and also had a specific fit to her role-relationship concepts. Her fear of humiliation, her interest in showing her good attributes, and her use of pretending as a defense were all heightened by recording the therapy. Janice had expectations of an audience watching the transactions from somewhere behind the therapist. She wondered how the therapist felt about being recorded and being so "onstage." He might be self-centered. In that way he could be seen as too much like her mother who, she felt, manipulated her to be "mother's own girl" and bolster her mother's image as "a good mother." If he were like her mother, the therapist would want her to submit and to cry so that he could exploit her emotional display as a sign of his good technique, just as she believed her mother did, in fact, want her to cry "appropriately" at the family gatherings discussing the ominous likely course of her brother's illness to demonstrate that her daughter—once too unconventional—now conformed to conventional behavior.

Change Process: Learning New Attitudes

The therapeutic alliance was gradually deepened and became much like the relationship of a slightly wayward student to a tolerant but firm teacher. For her, this was a freeing development. It was different from her parental relationships with a dogmatic father and an intrusive and demanding mother. She loved her parents, but ambivalently. She had to fight their injunctions to be like them and with them, as well as their criticisms or hurt feelings when she was unlike or away from them. With the therapist, she acknowledged her personal limitations while he protected her from

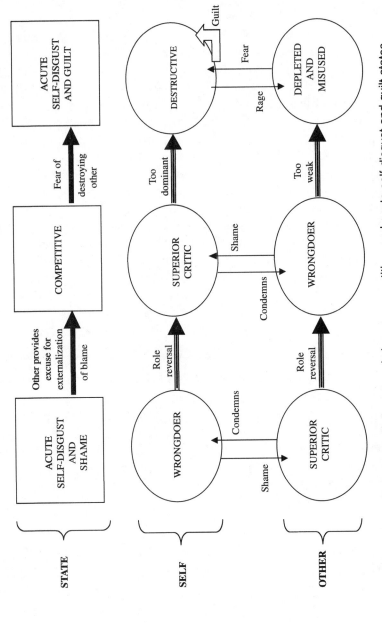

Figure 6.2. Role relationship for the acute self-disgust and shame, competitive, and acute self-disgust and guilt states.

excessive self-criticism, shame, and guilt. Together, they confronted some of her difficulties in making responsible decisions for her own life.

The principal difficulty in establishing this therapeutic relationship was Janice's aversion to presenting information that made her appear impaired, which led to her habitual style of pretense. In therapy, this manifested itself as pretending to be happy and satisfied, as resisting by attempting to establish an intellectual–social relationship, and as avoiding a therapeutic focus.

Once Janice's marked avoidances were counteracted, repeated discussions of the homesickness topic bolstered her autonomous intentions and her relatively competent self-concepts. She thought more clearly about her ambivalence toward her mother and disentangled this complex theme from her own shock and grief about eventually losing her brother. This made her less frightened of mourning. Her hopes for the future improved, and she was able to discuss how she could master a separation from the unsatisfactory relationship with Phillip. She also was able to make herself work well enough to retain her job until she could choose a better route to advancing her career.

CONCLUSION

In general, with many patients interactions with the therapist, as well as altered behavior patterns with others, are examined during this step of CA. The goal is fostering change in conscious attitudes about people and the self. Such modifications, when combined with trial and then repetition of new patterns of transaction, can gradually alter less conscious beliefs and person schemas.

The observations that are important in formulating how to best facilitate such processes of change are usually made from one or more of three types of stories of what happens between self and others. The same maladaptive cycle may be noted in these aspects of a triangle: (a) the inside-of-therapy relationships, (b) current relationships outside of therapy relationships, and (c) past relationships. The focus is on opportunities for better future relationships.

The inside-of-therapy relationships also come in a set of three forms worth looking for: (a) the therapeutic alliance, (b) the transference and countertransference alliances or enactments, and (c) defensive efforts to stabilize safety by evoking a social but not necessarily transferential alliance.

Awareness, **insight,** and new decisions help in altering relationship patterns from less to more adaptive. These processes also help in integrating attitudes that have been disjointed. The patient learns how to contain efforts to both approach the other and assert the self when with the other.

This does not mean, however, that conscious efforts are paramount. There are, for example, words to describe the therapeutic alliance, but it also has its own music. Unconscious modifications of aims, skills, and values also occur as the patient learns from new experiences and from identification with models provided by the therapist.

III

EVALUATION AND TREATMENT OUTCOME

7

STEP 8: EVALUATING CHANGE

In describing treatment outcome, one repeats the aspects of configurational analysis (CA) from a new perspective. Usually, this occurs as termination is contemplated. Optimally, treatment outcome is evaluated a month or more after the conclusion of treatment. While the economic pressures mitigate against this apparent luxury, nothing could be more valuable to clinicians in training. I still ask my own patients to see me again, often without charge or expectation of insurance reimbursement, so I can learn not only what changes during psychotherapy but what continues to change afterward.

Let us begin with a quick review of Janice's last three therapy sessions and her subsequent evaluation interviews. Janice began the 10th session by saying that she had been feeling better and more optimistic. She had gone to see an aunt and, while with her, Janice felt for the first time a sense of mutual intimacy with a senior family member, unlike feelings when with her mother or father. She then talked clearly with the therapist about how inappropriate her behavior had been during her brother's hospitalization; she described how silly she had acted and how she withdrew from others when she should have been supporting her parents and relatives. Her defensiveness was greatly diminished. The therapist aimed at making the following clarifications: Janice had feelings of shame and guilt because she had not expressed sadness to her fellow family members about her brother's dire prognosis; instead she had expressed a kind of passive–aggressive hostility toward her mother, especially as, in her view, her mother had used her brother's illness to seek sympathy for herself.

In the 11th interview, Janice reviewed this same material and focused on her ambivalent relationship with her mother. The therapist narrowed this down by helping her to look at a detailed reconstruction of interactions with her mother during her brother's hospitalization. Impending termination at the close of the next session was discussed.

Janice seemed poised and businesslike at the final interview, more distant from the therapist than during hours 8 through 11. She reviewed main themes. There was agreement that there had been a good therapeutic outcome.

She returned for a posttherapy evaluation 3 months later. She felt treatment had helped her considerably, she felt more stable and less depressed, with improved capacities at work. A second posttherapy evaluation session was conducted 10 months after termination. Janice described additional positive changes in her life. She had a clear feeling of increased control and improved (more continuous) self-esteem. Depressive episodes remained less frequent and more attenuated than before treatment. She had continued to improve in her work and had been praised and rewarded. In addition, she had made plans for advanced education.

She had separated amicably from Phillip and was living independently, only seeing him occasionally. She felt good about her decreased dependence on others and had renewed a close relationship with a female friend. She also felt increasingly adultlike in her relationship to her parents and planned to visit them in the near future. Her brother's condition had predictably worsened and she felt the need to be with him before he died. She thought she might seek more therapy in the future because she wanted to do more work on developmental issues and to seek support in mourning.

OVERVIEW OF STEP 8: EVALUATING CHANGE

The method of evaluating change is like the system for formulating what one might be able to change initially. It starts at the surface and proceeds to deeper levels of inference, looking as much as possible for clearly observable evidence. The comparison with initial judgments is helpful in this regard, because measuring patient satisfaction alone is not enough.

Phenomena and States of Mind

Describe outcome in terms of change from the items listed as phenomena in Step 1. Include examination of the effects of external changes, including shifts in family, social, and environmental contexts. Discuss new states and improvements or modifications of maladaptive state cycles with the patient. Compare the actual outcome with initial hopes and discuss possible future work by the patient. Consider the advisability of follow-up, booster sessions, and other options.

Topics of Concern

Describe outcome in terms of changes in the topics of concern. Indicate resolutions of conflicts as well as residual problematic themes and continued styles of dysfunctional avoidance or distortion. Discuss residual conflicted themes for self-work.

Identity and Relationships

Describe changes (or persistence) in maladaptive personality traits. Include modifications in enduring attitudes and personal agendas. Clarify with the patient where to focus to solidify gains and what to expect in the future. For example, therapy may start but not complete a normal process of seeking intimacy, taking on new skills for work, and mourning losses of the past, including lost ideals of finding perfect resolutions.

CHANGES IN PHENOMENA AND STATES OF MIND

Although patients and therapists alike desire total cure and remarkable advances in personal development, that is not the usual outcome of psychotherapy. More frequently, in a good outcome, problems are attenuated, coping styles improve, and self-esteem increases. Symptoms diminish in frequency and intensity but may not totally disappear. A person may markedly improve from a condition of continuous depression and still have moments of morbid self-reflection and gloom without being overwhelmed. As therapists, we need ways of specifying such typical results; state analysis is particularly useful for this purpose.

As mentioned in chapter 2, state analysis is a realistic way of estimating change; it illustrates how intensely and frequently a few defined states occur and with what degree of felt self-control. A person may, for example, have begun therapy with frequent experiences of undermodulated states of terror of job loss and end therapy with only well-modulated states of apprehension about job loss—an improvement even if fear of job loss remains present in that person's life. A person who was often in depressed states could, after therapy, be far less often in such states and more often in states of satisfaction, even if he or she still had occasional transient periods of self-criticism, pessimism, and gloom.

Of course, one hopes that the outcome is not just reduction of negative states but also enhancement of positive ones. Clinicians should assess outcome in terms of both types of states and modifications made in conflicted topics, habitual compensatory or coping strategies, and core schemas of self and others.

CASE EXAMPLE

Before therapy, Janice felt her greatest acute emotional distress during periods of self-disgust and chronic distress in her depressed, hurt and not working state. Her self-report of depression, on quantitative rating scales, had declined by the end of therapy, and she told the therapist that states of self-disgust occurred less frequently. During the 10 months that followed therapy, they were also less frequent, as indicated at the subsequent evaluation.

During the posttherapy period, there were other signs of positive change in states. She cried less often and entered the hurt and not working state less frequently. She spent more time in a working state, during which she felt less hurt. In addition, her competitive state was somewhat more in control, and the quality of this state changed. When in this state, she did not yield to impulsive outbursts of temper but was able to continue effective interchanges with the challenging person. The result was improved work performance and more rewards from her colleagues.

Her tra-la-la state remained frequent, but the quality of this state changed. She experienced herself as more authentic, a movement in the direction of a competent state she was not yet able to stabilize.

Janice felt transitions between states to be less passive and happenstance. She was aware of her states and often could control herself at points of likely transition to unwanted states. For example, during the first posttherapy evaluation interview, she said, "I feel, from the therapy and from the time that has gone by, that I've reached more of an equilibrium. Even now, when I'm in a mood, I can see a reason for it." Later in that interview, after the evaluator asked her to comment specifically on her moods, she said, "I feel like it's more of an equilibrium. It's settled into a comfortable, fairly content thing. And it goes up and down from there, always returning to there instead of me feeling devastated or frantic."

Her fear that the improvement might be transient is reflected in the following comment on her relationship with a supervisor at work:

P: I feel like last spring I had so much trouble with the woman that I was working under because of that emotional instability. I mean, I just couldn't react safely to people. And this year I'm just crossing my fingers out of a superstitious fear that it might happen again. I'm working under a different woman and it's going fantastically. I feel more confident and I'm doing a better job. This woman last year, her complaints were not entirely groundless, even though I reacted at first as if they were. But, I feel like I'm just more together and able to give more, and be more aware and on top of things. I don't know how long it will last.

She also said, "I was out of control [before therapy] and there were all these signs and I'm . . . I'm seeing that in her now [a friend who seems out of control] and it reminds me, at the same time, it makes me feel really good for not being there [out of control] anymore."

She kept her more adaptive perspective over the months that followed therapy, and her confidence in her control increased. For example, in the later evaluation interview she said, "I've just become a lot stronger . . . [even] when I feel tired and depressed. . . . I can see that as temporary."

To summarize, positive outcome was evident in the reduced frequency of entry into the states of self-disgust, crying, and hurt and not working. The quality of the hurt but working state changed so that the hurt quality diminished. The quality of the competitive state changed, with a less strident struggle to avoid submission by becoming dominant. The quality of the tra-la-la state changed: There was less feeling of pretending and lack of authenticity.

Overall, extremes were reduced and there was more control of state transitions. She had not yet achieved the desired state in which she would have a sense of personal integrity, competence, and mutuality, but she felt closer to that goal. Nor had she completely removed herself from the danger of self-disgust; however, she felt more confident and distant from the threat of searing shame. She was able to work on career and self-developmental plans. There was no worsening of any aspect of her condition.

CHANGE IN TOPICS OF CONCERN

In this step of CA, the clinician evaluates the modifications of beliefs and resolution of conflicts that have occurred in topics of concern. Shifts in basic premises lead, in part, to the changes in emotional states already described. **Themes** once accompanied by turbulent feeling may now be contemplated calmly. For example, memories of loss may have become desensitized so that the patient experiences sad nostalgia rather than violent pangs of agony. Ideas of loving or creating once expressed with intellectual detachment may now be expressed with feeling. The quality and intensity of emotions may change.

Altered controls of emotional information processing should also be described. Has there been an improvement of direct expression? Are ideas that were once so intrusive that they disrupted concentration now less peremptory? Can the previously unthinkable now be contemplated? Can the person, for example, both recall a traumatic memory and put it out of mind for a time?

Change may also be described in terms of any enhanced abilities to organize sequences of rational and coherent meaning. A person may have learned to think more in cause-and-effect sequences and to think in a more adaptive way before acting. These skills may be generalized from particular topics and become generally useful in living life well. Bodily communications once transmitted unknowingly may now be part of known and deliberate expression.

CASE EXAMPLE

For Janice, the topics of concern during therapy were centered on themes of her present status and future aims as an independent person, particularly in relation to her brother's illness, her return home, and nonfamily interactions during her visit home. At treatment onset, she was unable to fully contemplate her feelings about her brother's illness. She felt that she was floundering with impaired ability to think through her plans and with conflicted intentions, beliefs, and values about returning home or staying away, about separation from Phillip, and about identification with her mother.

One outcome of therapy was her increased ability to deploy direct, rational thinking about these topics. Relevant memories, associations, and feelings could at outcome of therapy be consciously contemplated with appropriate emotional expression. Although the constellation around personal independence-freeing strivings was not completely worked through, her movement toward this goal was significant.

Despite her difficulties in focusing on it early in therapy, she felt that her reactions to her brother's eventual death were the feelings most resolved at the end of treatment. She said the following in the last therapy hour:

> P: It's kind of funny: One of the things I feel most finished about is what I said I came in here for, which is about Sam's illness. I mean, all this time I've come to be much more accepting about my feelings about his illness. I still dream about him as he was before, but I've been glad dreaming about him. I've been glad to be getting flashes of him, because it hasn't been with that feeling of avoidance, instant rejection, and everything.

Toward the end of treatment and in the later evaluation sessions, she seemed more aware of her communications, more open to ideas, and richer in terms of experienced and expressed emotionality. These changes were probably a result of reduction in her habitual avoidance and thought-inhibition patterns. She had increased tolerance for sadness without concomitant feelings of helplessness and hopelessness.

She began therapy with a complex defensive style: She went beyond suppression to use disavowal, intellectualization, generalization, externalization, and switching maneuvers as ways to avoid dreaded emotional states. She used these defenses less in the final therapy sessions; this change was probably a result of an increased sense of safety provided by the therapeutic alliance and the interventions of the therapist to counteract her defenses. There were gains in her use of such conscious coping strategies as doing, deciding, being objective, analyzing situations, and making step-by-step decisions. This reduction in defensive emotional control processes allowed her to integrate her memory of her behavior when Sam was hospitalized, as well as anticipatory grief about his likely premature death.

In Janice's outcome evaluation session 3 months after therapy, she indicated this increase in insight about her responses during her visit home when Sam was hospitalized for the first time. For example, she said, "I just . . . wouldn't cry when others in the family did. It was because I didn't want to play their game. I didn't want to be sucked back in. I'm still—I'm still trying to—to be apart and be myself. And so I couldn't really let go."

MODIFICATION OF SELF-CONCEPTS AND ROLE-RELATIONSHIP MODELS

As the final part of outcome evaluation one can compare late-in-therapy and posttherapy interpersonal patterns with the pretherapy or early-in-therapy experiences. What maladaptive patterns ceased? What adaptive patterns developed? What stayed the same? Many patients—in fact, most people—have internal contradictions in how they view self and others. Have these configurations of belief been better harmonized and integrated within overall **self-organization** (Horowitz, 2002b)?

The ultimate test of any durable change is to be found in patterns that emerge after therapy. This is the period in which the patient is without the regular support of the therapist. The person should be better able to act competently, feel worthwhile, and experience intimate relationships on his or her own. For example, suppose a person complained of being depressed about his or her inability to sustain any significant relationship. A valuable outcome would be to have the ability to maintain a friendship, sexual liaison, marriage, care-taking, or collegial affiliation.

CASE EXAMPLE

An important adaptive self-concept was for Janice to view herself as a young adult learning about life and making new, clearer choices. This self-concept as student of life was used in the role-relationship model of the therapeutic alliance, with the therapist in a transient role as mentor. Unlike a dreaded role relationship with her mother, she saw herself as growing in therapy rather than replicating her mother or serving as her mother's appendage. The therapist was seen as encouraging rather than discouraging individuation. He was not fostering dependency. The principal change in self-images, in terms of outcome, was stabilization of this competent adult rather than childlike or adolescent self-concept.

Janice was able to move beyond her initial fear that she was being either too much like or too rebelliously different from her mother. She remained away from home and made choices that would gradually improve her career. She created and sustained relationships with women friends. She separated from Phillip, moved into her own apartment, and was glad that she did not then feel intolerably lonely, as she had feared. Ten months after therapy, during the posttherapy evaluation, Janice was also well into the process of recognizing the loss of her principal ally, her brother, in being independent of her mother. She was going through the normal healing process of anticipatory mourning.

Stabilization of her self-concept as a person learning to become more competent, creative, and womanly meant Janice became less vulnerable to dreaded states of mind organized by bad or worthless self-schema images. She also became less liable to use compensatory states organized by a role for self as a harsh, superior critic of others. This modification in self-organization meant less pretense at being an ideal woman and less vulnerability to shame if and when this pretense failed.

Her stabilized self-organization and more realistic models of relationships manifested themselves in reduced maladaptive behavior. After therapy, Janice was better able to tolerate her economically necessary subordinate position at work without feeling degraded and without behaving in a self-impairing indignant manner. She was able to get closer to her supervisor, an older woman, without rebelling on the one hand or feeling submerged or smothered on the other hand. She was also able to look for more training and aimed toward a better job.

She could tolerate not being at home, being far from old friends, and leaving Phillip without feeling excessively needy, lonely, or deprived. She was able to tolerate the absence of the therapeutic alliance without relapse into depression, a relapse she had feared toward the end of therapy. These gains put her at a greater distance from her fears of stagnation, defectiveness, and dependency.

It was clear that her gains fell short of her ideal goals, however. She did not maintain the weight loss begun during therapy, she had not arrived at a love relationship that was fulfilling, and she had not developed her creativity and work capacities to the degree she desired. She felt that she was "on her way" but was "uncertain of her stability" in spite of her increased sense of confidence and stability in herself as a person learning and gaining from life experiences.

These formulations are illustrated with excerpts. In the last treatment hour, she reviewed her gains and told the therapist that she feared that the loss of the therapeutic alliance could lead to a regression to her initial apathy and depression.

P: When you reminded me two or three sessions ago that we only had a few weeks left, I was really horrified: oh, God, no, we can't stop, I'll be lost and . . . But now I started thinking, maybe I'd like to try it by myself for awhile.

In an evaluation session 3 months after therapy, a different evaluating clinician spoke to Janice:

E: Do you feel like your life changed much during or after the period that you were in therapy?

P: Yes, I do, a lot. I feel like when I came in and for most of the time that I was in therapy, I was really upset about a lot of things and shaky and unstable. And I, I felt very, very out of control. Moods would come and I had no idea where they had come from or what to do about them. Kind of falling over cliffs all the time. And I don't feel that way anymore. I feel like from the therapy and from the time that has gone by, I've reached a lot more of equilibrium and even now, when I'm in a mood, I can see a reason for it.

E: You're feeling more in control of your feelings?

P: I am. And of my environment. And I feel like last spring, I had so much trouble with the woman that I was working under, partially because of that emotional instability. I mean, I just couldn't react safely to people, and this year I'm just crossing my fingers out of superstitious fear that it might happen again. I'm working under a different woman and it's going fantastic.

The process of improvement in her self-concepts and self-experiences continued, and at evaluation of her status 10 months after therapy, Janice told the evaluating clinician:

P: I feel a lot more in control of myself and of my life than I did then—not just thrown by his [her brother's] illness, but just power-less in general. Like, everything kind of fell apart and I feel like I'm . . . I know what direction I'm going in [now]. I have plans, and I'm more able to deal with daily crises and stuff and, in fact, I'm dealing with a major crisis in a way that I'm feeling pretty good about. The major crisis was when I left my Phillip, the guy that I lived with.

E: Even in crises, you still have some sense of control?

P: I, right. I feel like I, you know, I, er, even though, even when I'm aware of being really confused or depressed, I have a little more sense of me-ness and of liking the me and just since talking to you and making this last appointment I have obviously been thinking about what's happening, and I've just been really pleased about it.

Later, while talking specifically about the decision to leave Phillip, the evaluating clinician confronted her with her previous worry about being too dependent:

E: What's your sense of what's changed? I remember the last time I talked to you, it was your feeling that you were a little uncomfortable about that relationship with Phillip, that you didn't want to examine it because you were afraid of what you might find.

P: I'm feeling so much better about myself that I don't need as much security, and I'm more able to face the things I don't like about the relationship. I demand a lot out of any relationship. I mean this is one thing that bugs me; I feel like I'm a failure at relationships. I can never have one that lasts for longer than a year. I'll probably be an old maid all my life because I can't live with people—just impossible. And I, I say that all facetiously. [This is a bit of a return of the tra-la-la state.]

E: But those are thoughts you've been having?

P: But those are thoughts I've been having, yeah. Anyway, one of the things I do want to change is I want to be able to learn, not so much to be more objective, but to know what to do with all my emotions. I want to be able to take things easy a little bit more. If I hadn't been demanding so much of Phillip, I wouldn't have been so bothered when he ignored me. Of course, you can say that a different way; you could say if I hadn't cared so much for him, I wouldn't have been so bothered. I mean if I didn't give a damn about him, I wouldn't give a damn what he did.

I've been thinking. Maybe a group would be better and a good thing if and when I want more therapy, because it would be less like going to a shrink. And there'd be the perceptions of other people. It wouldn't be the choice between your opinion and my opinion or something like that. Yeah. I really liked my therapist's objectivity. I felt myself being able to just be myself instead of trying to impress him or trying to win his sympathy or anything. And I imagine a group wouldn't be able to do for me as much as he did.

On the other hand, one of the things I want right now is to find out what I believe about a lot of things, you know, whether I actually believe this or whether I've just been kind of conditioned to believe it, by (a) my parents or (b) my peers. If I have a bunch of different opinions, then maybe I can use bunches of people as sounding boards and, either in agreement or in contradiction, and find out what I think.

One may infer from these statements that Janice improved her self-concept as capable of autonomy and independence but that there was residual worry. In other words, a central problem theme before therapy had a more advanced configuration after therapy, and she was still at work—and ready to seek more help on—her personal development. She felt hopeful about her journey.

For Janice, testing the therapist and the eventual development of a therapeutic alliance seemed to be an important process that led to her improvement. To her, it meant that in psychotherapy, she could work on organizing her immediate life, with a sense of safety about relating to a person seen as helpful but not demanding her subordination. She could bear being helped by a person not overly concerned or dependent on her. The therapeutic alliance encouraged her, allowed her to begin to resolve her responses to the illness of her brother, and sustained her temporarily in an identity crisis, allowing continued personal efforts toward decision making, independence, and learning of skills.

The most important gain, with regard to her self-concept, came from realizing that she could both participate in therapy and tolerate separation from it and from the therapist. These ideational processes led to a major shift in the direction of experiencing herself as less dependent and more competent. Continued work on her own or in therapy might help to solidify this goal of personal development.

CONCLUSION

The series of self–other concepts described for the pretherapy period can be compared with the series of self-concepts and patterns of relating to others as experienced or manifested during the posttherapy period. The qualities of self-concept, the solidity and continuity of a sense of identity, the coherence in self-organization over time, and the degree of felt control and valuation are all important to note.

We have now completed CA. One illustrative case was presented for each of the eight steps. In the next chapter, for purposes of review, I present a briefer case example of a patient I call Connie.

8

REVIEW OF CONFIGURATIONAL ANALYSIS

This chapter provides one brief case study for the purposes of reviewing configurational analysis (CA) in brief psychotherapy.

CONNIE: A CONCISE FORMULATION OF WHAT CHANGED IN PSYCHOTHERAPY

Connie was a 28-year-old single woman living on unemployment insurance while living with friends when she began therapy. She brought herself to therapy because she was distressed about her inability to work, intrusive crying, and mixed anxious and depressed feelings related to the death of her father 5 weeks earlier. After evaluation, she was seen in weekly, individual psychotherapy for 3 months.

Phenomena

After the death of her father, Connie's creative work and searches for employment stopped. She complained of intrusive episodes of crying, which she attempted to stifle. She concealed from others that these were instigated by her thoughts about her father. During conversations, she was unable to follow the thread of topics and instead felt inwardly dazed. She was frightened by these symptoms and states, in which she had diminished control over herself. She was preoccupied with thoughts of death and, in addition to the sudden outbursts of sadness, she felt a sense of lack of direction in her life. Most of these symptoms disappeared at the time of a follow-up interview that was conducted by an evaluating clinician 3 months after the end of therapy.

States

The most upsetting problem state was intensive crying. She dreaded another descent into apathetic despair or a state in which she felt as-if crazy. These interfered with the desired states of composed creativity when alone and mutuality when with others. She had a protective compromise, an as-if composed state, which seemed inauthentic to the therapist. A more problematic compromise, the distracted state, occurred and interrupted work and relationships outside of therapy, and it also occurred in therapy sessions.

Topics of Concern and Defensive Control Processes

The death of Connie's father set in motion a train of thought to redefine the story of her relationship with him. Connie had important memories of idealized, happy times in his company. These were periods of apparently mutual admiration. But, after she sided with him in his divorce conflict with her mother, he became remote and then Connie was shocked when he married a woman younger than himself.

Connie interpreted his remarriage and then his death as if both were rejections of her. His death was also a final loss of the chance to regain his admiration. She also felt as if dying his punishment for rejecting her. That is, his premature and unexpected stroke was seen by Connie as a psychosomatic response to his recognition that he had destroyed a meaningful attachment. When she began to experience resentment, however, she had to inhibit these ideas because of a **magical belief** that her anger harmed him. When she could not inhibit these magical and irrational ideas, she tended to enter into altered states of consciousness such as the distracted state.

Relationships

Connie was vulnerable to defective self-concepts, especially around her vocational identity or sense of competence. In college, she had followed her father's suggestions about what subject to major in, which was business. After college, she obtained work as a minor bank executive. She felt that this job was a dead end, and her lack of more advanced skills made her feel relatively worthless. She left her place of employment so that she could have a period in which to reorient her values and develop her skills in creative arts. During this time, when she was evaluating her life, her father died. His death meant the interruption of her plan: He would not come to see that she was a worthwhile person, and thus she was not able to revise the rejection she had felt for the past 5 years and thus restore her early adolescent relationship of mutual admiration and even adoration.

Her father's rejection of her was mysterious and unexplained even before his death. In fact, the last time Connie had seen her father was part of an effort by her to regain the positive and secure attachment of her earlier adolescence or at least to find out the reasons for his neglect and remoteness. She had come to appraise her father as a cold, selfish man who had, in a way, tricked and used her in his eventual divorce from her mother; he then neglected and showed that he no longer needed her when he married a woman much younger than himself with whom he then had a child. She experienced these actions as a result of his scorn for her and felt herself to be either defective or unfairly rejected.

Her father wanted a divorce because of the mother's frequent out-of-control rages and crying spells. Connie feared that by expressing anger, fear, and sadness after his death in undermodulated states of mind, she would appear to be too much like her mother. She dreaded being viewed as a "messy emotionalist," a harshly critical view of her mother that she shared with her father.

PROCESS OF THERAPY

The now familiar CA headings of states, topics of concern, and defensive control processes and relationships are then repeated to examine the therapy interactions.

States

Connie had intrusive crying during the evaluation interview with a woman clinician but warded off crying while talking during the first session with the male therapist. The therapist detected her inhibition. He told her that he would not feel critical of her if she did cry. She gradually became able to engage in open crying. As she worked through themes of mourning and of resentment toward her father, she was able to engage more of the time in a working state, expressing emotions with fewer feelings of being out of control.

Because the therapist was helpful, she at first sometimes saw him as an ideal father reestablishing the lost ideal relationship. During some episodes of this positive transference, she exhibited a shining state, which was like the one previously referred to as mutual admiration with her father. She also was occasionally skeptical and challenging of the therapist in mild trials to determine whether he could safely tolerate resentment and the possibility of a negative transference.

Early in therapy, there was a phase—repeated occasionally in later hours—in which she would begin each interview in the distracted state, not knowing what to say; this seemed to be a testing period. A therapeutic alliance, however, was soon established and working states ensued. There were some well-modulated sad states in the concluding sessions.

Topics of Concern and Defensive Control Processes

The main theme explored during therapy was the need to understand the meaning of her father's rejection of her. As the therapist began to counter some of her defensive inhibitions and denials, Connie was gradually able to get in touch with her resentment toward her father and her feelings of weakness and degradation. Emergence of her past history over the first series of sessions led to a gradual increase in focus on the present and future aspects of the therapy.

One of the important future themes interpreted by the therapist was Connie's tendency to repeat the relationship with her father in her romantic selection of older men whom she could idealize but who then turned out to be cold and remote. It seemed that the death of her father also created a pivotal point at which she might reject men altogether, as individuals who were incapable of returning love and care. Another version of this theme was the need to rescue lonely men; she showed some regret that she had failed to rescue her father from what she saw as a psychosomatic illness.

Relationships

The therapeutic alliance seemed to be merged with a positive transference right away because of Connie's intense need. As her symptoms decreased rapidly over the first few sessions, however, Connie began to test the therapist. The critical issue was whether the therapist would see her as worthwhile or worthless because of some of her nonconformity with what she supposed (correctly) were his social values. Her countercultural attitudes were rebellious against her father, who disapproved of her behaviors. As she found that the therapist did not degrade her values, an increase in her self-esteem and her trust of the therapeutic alliance resulted. As Connie's self-esteem increased, she was more willing to accept the challenge of additional exploration of her ideas and feelings, leading to more insight and new decision making.

STEP 8: EVALUATION OF THE OUTCOME OF CONNIE'S TREATMENT

At a 3-month follow-up session, Connie was no longer having the symptomatic undermodulated states of intrusive crying. Distraught states occurred only rarely and then briefly. She was less depressed and felt generally more purposeful and able to have long periods in which she felt stable in a working state.

Topics of Concern and Defensive Control Processes

The major change in the status of ideas was the development of a concept of the historical evolution and meaning of her relationship with her father. Connie had integrated various self-images and relationship models so that she now had a central view of him not as cold and rejecting but rather as a person who had multiple self-images: as needing her while contradictorily standing aloof and expressing an absence of need, as telling her to be independent while covertly telling her to remain tied to him. The premise that she could not feel angry with her father for being neurotically conflicted was altered; she now believed it was acceptable to express anger with him and with related male figures. Because of these changes, she could allow herself to progress through waves of grief work characteristic of mourning.

In addition, she was able to differentiate her fear of weakness, sadness at loss, resentment at scorn, and remoteness from "messy emotions," while concurrently developing a more complex, less stereotyped view of her mother.

Relationships

Connie felt an increased sense of self-worth. This was seen as a shift back to a position present before the father's death rather than a new development. At the follow-up, she was still very much engaged in reviewing the meaning of her father's death and accepting the mourning process without fear or blocking. She was considering new relationships and had embarked on a new romantic attachment with less projection and more attention to his actual qualities.

CONCLUSION

The kind of case write-up presented in this chapter is a valuable record. If and when Connie took an opportunity to engage in additional psychotherapeutic work it would be a good thing for a clinician to read. Beyond this function as a good type of summary, doing such write-ups about change is a form of continuing growth in clarity, understanding, and knowledge for the clinician who does it with care, openness, and a questioning attitude.

CA is a simple format to keep in mind for your future work: Just memorize a triad of (a) states of mind, (b) topics and defenses or avoidances, and (c) schemas of self and other. This triad is then examined in terms of an initial evaluative formulation, an in-process reappraisal, and from an outcome-oriented (change) perspective. To avoid diffusion it is helpful to begin a write-up by stating the initial phenomena, usually signs–symptoms–problems-in-living, that you will focus on explaining.

With a few repetitions you can make this a personal framework, altering the approach as you wish and individualizing it to fit your particular and unique client or patient. I hope you and that person you provide with care will both find the experience rewarding.

EPILOGUE

The best way to continue to learn to use configurational analysis (CA) is to apply it to a case you know pretty well. It may help to go back and review the illustrative case for states before (chap. 2, this volume), during (chap. 5, this volume), and after therapy (chap. 7, this volume), then review for topics and controls before (chap. 3, this volume), in process (chap. 5, this volume), and at outcome (chap. 7, this volume). Finally, you can look again at chapters that say how to infer roles of self-and-other from the evaluation (chap. 4, this volume), therapy (chap. 6, this volume), and outcome points of view (chap. 7, this volume).

If one does not formulate a case for a long period of time, even after learning how for the first time, one can get rusty or creaky. Starting out to formulate moves in fits and starts. The process gets smoother and eventually fluid. Formulation becomes intuitive except in difficult cases, where it becomes most valuable but also more effortful. The terrific advantage of formulation is that understanding flows easily into choice of technique, especially interventions that integrate tools learned from various earlier sources.

In the beginning, it is unlikely that a therapist in training can do CA while in a session with his or her patient. Quiet contemplation when alone is needed. That builds a skill that will gradually become more intuitive and that can be used more during sessions.

The therapist understands, imagines directions for change, and reacts seamlessly with the patient. It is the same way that one gets to Carnegie Hall: practice, practice, practice. What I mean is this: What feels awkward at first will soon be rewarding. The main principles are to start at the surface, observe for variations in state, and then find what explains the variations.

Then you can look for biopsychosocial interactions, including yourself in the equation as you examine process and consider how a current pattern developed. As you do so, consider the immediate future: asking when, where, and how can you help your patient next to change. I think you will find you also have changed.

GLOSSARY

Analysis: A process of describing parts, why they formed, how they fit together, and interact on each other.

Belief structures: The associational patterns that connect meanings and other elements of mental content.

Character: A complex belief structure of learned and enduring meanings that leads to identity patterns.

Configuration: A set of associatively related but possibly contradictory beliefs. Conflictual configurations have poorly integrated elements and harmonious ones have well-integrated elements.

Configurational analysis: A system of formulation that describes (a) the current phenomena to be explained, (b) state cycles in which the phenomena do and do not occur, (c) relevant themes and habitual defenses that ward off emotions and clarity, and (d) the configurations of person schemas that explain the current states and cycles.

Cycles: Repeated sequential patterns of mood and behavior states. Adaptive cycles allow people to behave appropriately. Maladaptive cycles disable people from behaving appropriately and expediently in a wide array of situations.

Defensive control processes: Mental activities, often operating unconsciously, that ward off dreaded states. These regulatory processes make use of the inhibitions and facilitations that can effect both the form and contents of thought as well as the schemas used to organize thought and action.

Identity: Awareness of the self as a continuous and, usually, coherent entity that perceives, thinks, feels, decides, and acts.

Insight: A realization about the cause and/or effect of a situation or the connection between elements in a pattern.

Magical belief: Thinking based in fantasy rather than reality.

Overmodulated states: Because of excessive defensive controls or habitual restrictive character traits, overmodulated states seem like a mask over true feelings and frank attitudes. The appearance is wooden, unauthentic, dry, or arch, but bantering and joking can also be found in an overmodulated state.

Person schema: A cognitive map of self, others, and attachments that operates as more than the sum of its parts; it is regarded as an organized whole. It might include body images, traits, roles, values, and mannerisms. The subordinate parts are beliefs that would nest in a hierarchy leading up to the whole. This whole is a working model of self, other or of a group of people are likely to interact.

Preconscious: Preparatory work that occurs with information before it is constructed into conscious representations.

Psychopathology: Psychiatric symptoms and problems based on mind–brain causations.

Psychotherapy: The clinical method in which a clinician supports and facilitates a patient's psychological and social efforts to overcome problems, conflicts, and inhibitions that impede optimum personal development.

Role-relationship models: Inner schemas and scripts blueprinting interpersonal transactions as well as views of self and others. Some role-relationship models are desired: They depict positive outcomes that a person seeks to achieve. Others are dreaded: They depict negative outcomes that a person seeks to avoid. Some role-relationship models are compromises to avoid wish–fear dilemmas. Of these, some are problematic compromise, containing symptom-causing elements, and others are protective compromises, containing coping or defensive elements.

Schema: A usually unconscious meaning that can serve as an organizer in the formation of thought. Schemas influence how motives reach awareness and action. They guide expectation and planning. Schemas tend to endure and change slowly as the integration of new understanding modifies earlier forms. Small-order schemas can be nested into hierarchies acting as larger order or supraordinate schemas.

Self-concept: Sense of "I" in a recurrent form that can be, and at least once has been, consciously experienced.

Self-objects: Other people or things that an individual views as an extension of him- or herself rather than a fully separate and autonomous person.

Self-organization: A person's overall set of available schemas and supraordinate schemas.

Self-schema: An unconscious organizer of many features into a holistic pattern. The term **self-schemas** can apply to enduring codifications and structure influencing thought, mood, and behavior. A self-schema will also influence formation of a sense of an identity.

Shimmering states: States characterized by signs of discord. The observed individual may shift rapidly between undercontrolled and overcontrolled emotional signals. The observer may recognize different signs in verbal and nonverbal modes. The clashing signals occur simultaneously or within a very brief period of time.

States: Combinations of conscious and unconscious experiences, with patterns of behavior that last for a period of time and that can be observed by others as having emotional, regulatory, and motivational qualities.

Supraordinate schema: A larger structure that uses associational beliefs to contain a hierarchy of multiple subordinate self-schemas. This larger form contains more than one self-schema. In other words, a self-schema is ordinate and several can be configured into a supraordinate schema.

Theme: A theme is usually large, complicated, and composed of varied topics. Narrative themes can represent complex patterns in a relationship and sense of personal destiny. Themes usually project into an anticipated future and root in the past.

Therapeutic alliance: The relationship that forms between a patient and a therapist, which allows them to work together toward a mutual goal.

Transaction: Communication or other behavior from one person to another. The term implies more than that in the context of psychotherapy, including, in its plural, a back and forth sequence, usually one person acting on another and receiving responses, as well as having reactions to those responses. One can have a cognitive map of expected and intended transactions and also a memory transcript or generalization schema of past transactions.

Transference: The displacement of ideas, feelings, motives, and actions associated with a previous relationship to a current relationship to a degree that the belief structure is, in part, inappropriate.

Undermodulated states: States that appear to the observer as if the individual has diminished self-regulation of emotional expression. This leads to appraisals of the individual as impulsive, uncontrolled, or experiencing intrusive feelings. The observer may experience surges of emotion as an empathic response or perhaps feel a wish to intervene in a way that will help the other gain control.

Well-modulated states: Such states exemplify a relatively smooth and harmonious flow of expressions. The observer appraises the individual as engaged in an organized process without major discords between verbal and nonverbal modes of expression. Affective displays appear genuine and, even when intense, are expressed in a poised manner. The observer may feel a sense of being well-connected to the expressed communications.

Working model: The currently active schematic organization of beliefs. A working model usually combines perceived information with information from activated, enduring schemas.

REFERENCES

Alexander, F., & French, T. (1946). *Psychoanalytic therapy: Principles and application*. New York: Ronald Press.

Arlow, J. (1969). Unconscious fantasy and disturbances of conscious experience. *Psychoanalytic Quarterly, 38*, 1–27.

Bannister, D. (Ed.). (1985). *Issues and approaches in personal construct theory*. London: Academic Press.

Bartlett, F. C. (1932). *Remembering: A study in experimental and social psychology*. Cambridge, England: Cambridge University Press.

Beck, A. T. (1976). *Cognitive therapy and the emotional disorders*. New York: International Universities Press.

Beck, A. T., & Emery, G. (1985). *Anxiety disorders and phobias: A cognitive perspective*. New York: Basic Books.

Benjamin, L. S. (1979). Use of structural analysis of social behavior (SASB) and Markov chains to study dyadic interactions. *Journal of Abnormal Psychology, 88*, 303–319.

Benjamin, L. S. (1993). *From interpersonal diagnosis to treatment, the SASB approach*. New York: Guilford Press.

Benjamin, L. S., & Friedrich, F. J. (1991). Contributions of structural analysis of social behavior (SASB) to the bridge between cognitive science and a science of object relations. In M. J. Horowitz (Ed.), *Person schemas and maladaptive interpersonal patterns* (pp. 379–412). Chicago: University of Chicago Press.

Berne, E. (1961). *Transactional analysis in psychotherapy*. New York: Grove Press.

Berne, E. (1964). *Games people play*. New York: Grove Press.

Bibring, E. (1953). The mechanism of depression. In P. Greenacre (Ed.), *Affective disorders* (pp. 13–48). New York: International Universities Press.

Bond, M., Gardner, S., Christian, J., & Sigal, J. S. (1983). Empirical study of self-rated defense styles. *Archives of General Psychiatry, 40*, 333–338.

Bower, G. H., Black, J. B., & Turner, T. J. (1979). Scripts in memory for text. *Cognitive Psychology, 11*, 117–120.

Bowlby, J. (1969). *Attachment and loss. Vol. 1: Attachment*. London: Hogarth Press.

Bowlby, J. (1973). *Attachment and loss. Vol. 2: Separation: Anxiety and anger*. New York: Basic Books.

Bowlby, J. (1980). *Attachment and loss. Vol. 3: Sadness and depression*. New York: Basic Books.

Breuer, J., & Freud, S. (1957). *Studies on hysteria* (2nd ed.). London: Hogarth Press. (Original work published 1895)

Carlson, R., & Carlson, L. (1984). Affect and psychological magnification: Derivations from Tomkins script theory. *Journal of Personality, 52*, 36–45.

Charcot, J. M. (1877). *Lectures on diseases of the nervous system* (Trans. G. Sigerson). London: New Sydenham Society. (Original work published 1877)

Curtis, J. D., Silberschatz, G., Sampson, H., Weiss, J., & Rosenberg, S. E. (1988). Developing reliable psychodynamic case formulations: An illustration of the plan diagnosis method. *Psychotherapy: Theory, research, practice, training* (Vol. 25, pp. 256–265). Washington, DC: American Psychological Association.

Eells, T. D. (Ed.). (1997). *Handbook of psychotherapy case formulation.* New York: Guilford Press.

Eells, T. D., Horowitz, M. J., Singer, J., Salovey, P., Daigle, D., & Turvey, C. (1995). The role relationship models method: A comparison of independently derived case formulations. *Psychotherapy Research, 5,* 161–175.

Erikson, E. (1954). The dream specimen of psychoanalysis. *Journal of the American Psychoanalytic Association, 2,* 5–55.

Federn, P. (1952). *Ego psychology and the psychosis.* New York: Basic Books.

Fiske, S. T., & Taylor, S. E. (1984). *Social cognition.* Reading, MA: Addison-Wesley.

Frank, J. D. (1974). Therapeutic components of psychotherapy. *Journal of Nervous and Mental Disease, 159,* 325–342.

Freud, A. (1936). *The ego and the mechanisms of defense.* London: Hogarth Press.

Freud, S. (1905). Three essays on the theory of sexuality. In *Standard edition* (Vol. 7). London: Hogarth Press.

Freud, S. (1955). The dynamics of transference. In J. Strachey (Ed.), *Standard edition* (Vol. 12, pp. 97–108). London: Hogarth. (Original work published 1912)

Gaarter, K. (1971). Control of states of consciousness: Attainment through external feedback augmenting control of psychophysiological variables. *Archives of General Psychiatry, 25,* 436–441.

Gill, M. M. (1982). Analysis of transference: Theory and technique. *Psychological Issues, 53,* 1–193.

Gill, M. M., & Hoffman, I. Z. (1982). Analysis of transference: II. Studies of nine audio-recorded psychoanalytic sessions. *Psychological Issues, 54,* 1–236.

Goldfried, M. R. (1995). *From cognitive–behavior therapy to psychotherapy integration: An evolving view.* New York: Springer.

Greenson, R. (1967). *Technique and practice of psychoanalysis.* New York: Hallmark Press.

Hartmann, H. (1950). Comments on psychoanalytic theory of the ego. In H. Hartmann (Ed.), *Essays in ego psychology: Selected problems in psychoanalytic theory* (pp. 113–141). New York: International Universities Press.

Hartocollis, P. (Ed.). (1977). *Borderline personality disorder.* New York: International Universities Press.

Horowitz, M. J. (1976). *Stress response syndromes.* Northvale, NJ: Aronson.

Horowitz, M. J. (1977). Structure and the process of change. In M. J. Horowitz (Ed.), *Hysterical personality* (pp. 329–399). New York: Aronson.

Horowitz, M. J. (1979). *States of mind.* New York: Plenum Press.

Horowitz, M. J. (1986). *Stress response syndromes* (2nd ed.). Northvale, NJ: Aronson.

Horowitz, M. J. (1987). *States of mind: Configurational analysis of individual psychology* (2nd ed.). New York: Plenum Press.

Horowitz, M. J. (1988a). *Introduction to psychodynamics: A new synthesis.* New York: Basic Books.

Horowitz, M. J. (Ed.). (1988b). *Psychodynamics and cognition.* Chicago: University of Chicago Press.

Horowitz, M. J. (1989). Relationship schema formulation: Role-relationship models and intrapsychic conflict. *Psychiatry, 52,* 260–274.

Horowitz, M. J. (1991a). *Hysterical personality and the histrionic personality disorder* (2nd ed.). Northvale, NJ: Aronson.

Horowitz, M. J. (1991b). *Person schemas and maladaptive interpersonal patterns.* Chicago: University of Chicago Press.

Horowitz, M. J. (1997). *Formulation as a basis for planning psychotherapy treatment.* Washington, DC: American Psychiatric Association.

Horowitz, M. J. (1998). *Cognitive psychodynamics: From conflict to character.* New York: Wiley.

Horowitz, M. J. (2001). *Stress response syndromes* (4th ed.). Northvale, NJ: Aronson.

Horowitz, M. J. (2002a). Configurational analysis. In M. Hersen & W. Sledge (Eds.), *Encyclopedia of psychotherapy* (Vol. 1, pp. 511–515). New York: Academic Press.

Horowitz, M. J. (2002b). Defining character integrity. *Journal of the American Psychoanalytic Association, 50,* 551–573.

Horowitz, M. J. (2002c). Self and relational observation. *Journal of Psychotherapy Integration, 12,* 115–127.

Horowitz, M. J. (2003). *Treatment of stress response syndromes.* Washington, DC: American Psychiatric Association.

Horowitz, M. J., & Eells, T. (1993). Case formulations using role-relationship model configurations: A reliability study. *Psychotherapy Research, 3,* 57–68.

Horowitz, M. J., Eells, T., Singer, J. L., & Salovey, P. (1995). Role-relationship models for case formulation. *Archives of General Psychiatry, 53,* 627–632.

Horowitz, M. J., Ewert, M., & Milbrath, C. M. (1996). States of emotional control during psychotherapy. *Journal of Psychotherapy Research and Practice, 5,* 20–25.

Horowitz, M. J., Kernberg, O., & Weinshel, E. (Eds.). (1993). *Psychic structure and change in psychoanalysis.* New York: International Universities Press.

Horowitz, M. J., Luborsky, L., & Popp, C. (1991). A comparison of the role-relationship models configuration and the core conflictual relationship theme. In M. J. Horowitz (Ed.), *Person schemas and maladaptive interpersonal patterns* (pp. 213–219). Chicago: University of Chicago Press.

Horowitz, M. J., Marmar, C., Krupnick, J., Wilner, N., Kaltreider, N., & Wallerstein, R. (1984). *Personality styles and brief psychotherapy.* New York: Basic Books.

Horowitz, M. J., Marmar, C., Weiss, D. S., DeWitt, K., & Rosenbaum, R. (1984). Brief psychotherapy of bereavement reactions: The relationship of process to outcome. *Archives of General Psychiatry, 41,* 438–448.

Horowitz, M. J., Marmar, C., & Wilner, N. (1979). Analysis of patient states and state transitions. *Journal of Nervous and Mental Disease, 167,* 91–99.

Horowitz, M. J., Merluzzi, T. V., Ewert, M., Ghannam, J. H., Hartley, D., & Stinson, C. (1991). Role-relationship models configuration. In M. J. Horowitz (Ed.), *Person schemas and maladaptive interpersonal patterns* (pp. 115–154). Chicago: University of Chicago Press.

Horowitz, M. J., Milbrath, C., Ewert, M., Sonneborn, D., & Stinson, C. H. (1994). Cyclical patterns of states of mind in psychotherapy. *American Journal of Psychiatry, 151,* 1767–1770.

Horowitz, M. J., Milbrath, C., Jordan, D. S., Stinson, C. H., Ewert, M., Redington, D. J., et al. (1994). Expressive and defensive behavior during discourse on unresolved topics: A single case study of pathological grief. *Journal of Personality, 62,* 527–563.

Horowitz, M. J., Milbrath, C., Reidbord, S., & Stinson, C. H. (1993). Elaboration and dyselaboration: Measures of expression and defense in discourse. *Psychotherapy Research, 3,* 278–293.

Horowitz, M. J., Milbrath C., & Stinson, C. (1995). Signs of defensive control locate conflicted topics in discourse. *Archives of General Psychiatry, 52,* 1040–1057.

Horowitz, M. J., & Stinson, C. H. (1995). Defenses as aspects of person schemas and control processes. In H. Conte & R. Plutchik (Eds.), *Ego defenses: Theory and measurement* (pp. 79–97). Oxford, England: Wiley.

Horowitz, M. J., Stinson, C. H., Curtis, D., Ewert, M., Redington, D., Singer, J. L., et al. (1993). Topics and signs: Defensive control of emotional expression. *Journal of Consulting and Clinical Psychology, 61,* 421–430.

Horowitz, M. J., Stinson, C. H., Fridhandler, B., Ewert, M., Milbrath, C., & Redington, D. (1993). Pathological grief: An intensive case study. *Psychiatry, 56,* 356–374.

Horowitz, M. J., Stinson, C. H., & Milbrath, C. (1996). Role relationship models: A person schematic method for inferring beliefs about identity and social action. In A. Colby, R. Jessor, & R. Shweder (Eds.), *Ethnography and human development* (pp. 253–274). Chicago: University of Chicago Press.

Horowitz, M. J., & Zilberg, N. (1983). Regressive alterations in the self-concept. *American Journal of Psychiatry, 140,* 284–289.

Horowitz, M. J., Znoj, H., & Stinson, C. (1996). Defensive control processes: Use of theory in research, formulation, and therapy of stress response syndromes. In M. Zeidner & N. Endler (Eds.), *Handbook of coping* (pp. 532–553). New York: Wiley.

Jacobson, E. (1964). *The self and object world.* New York: International Universities Press.

Janet, P. (1965). *The major symptoms of hysteria.* New York: Hafner.

Janis, I. (1969). *Stress and frustration*. New York: Harcourt Brace Jovanovich.

Johnson, S. M. (1994). *Character styles*. New York: W. W. Norton.

Kagan, R. (1982). *The developing self*. Cambridge, MA: Harvard University Press.

Kelly, G. A. (1955). *The psychology of personal constructs*. New York: Norton.

Kernberg, O. F. (1967). Borderline personality organization. *Journal of the American Psychoanalytic Association, 15*, 41–68.

Kernberg, O. F. (1975). *Borderline conditions and pathological narcissism*. New York: Aronson.

Kernberg, O. F. (1984). *Object-relations theory and clinical psychoanalysis*. New York: Aronson.

Kiesler, D. J. (1983). The 1982 interpersonal circle: A taxonomy for complimentarity in human transactions. *Psychological Review, 90*, 185–214.

Kihlstrom, J., & Cantor, N. (1984). Mental representations of self. In L. Berkowitz (Ed.), *Advances in experimental social psychology* (pp. 1–47). New York: Academic Press.

Klein, M. (1948). *Contribution to psychoanalysis*. London: Hogarth Press.

Knapp, P. H. (1969). Image, symbol and person. *Archives of General Psychiatry, 21*, 392–406.

Kohut, H. (1971). *Analysis of the self*. New York: International Universities Press.

Kohut, H. (1977). *Restoration of the self*. New York: International Universities Press.

Kohut, H. (1978). *The search for the self: Selected writings of Heinz Kohut*. New York: International Universities Press.

Langs, R. (1976). *The therapeutic interaction*. New York: Aronson.

Lazarus, R. S., & Folkman, S. (1984). *Stress, appraisal and coping*. New York: Springer.

Loevinger, J. (1976). *Ego development*. San Francisco: Jossey-Bass.

Loewald, H. (1960). On the therapeutic action of psychoanalysis. *International Journal of Psycho-Analysis, 24*, 16–33.

Luborsky, L. (1977). Measuring a pervasive psychic structure in psychotherapy: The core conflictual relationship theme. In N. Freedman & S. S. Grand (Eds.), *Communicative structures and psychic structures* (pp. 367–395). New York: Plenum Press.

Luborsky, L. (1984). *Principles of psychoanalytic psychotherapy: A manual for supportive expressive treatment*. New York: Basic Books.

Luborsky, L., & Crits-Christoph, P. (1990). *Understanding transference: The core conflictual relationship theme model*. New York: Basic Books.

Markus, H. (1977). Self-schemata and processing information about the self. *Journal of Personality and Social Psychology, 35*, 63–78.

Markus, H., & Smith, J. (1981). The influence of self-schemata on the perception of others. In N. Cantor & J. F. Kihlstrom (Eds.), *Personality, cognition and social interaction* (pp. 233–262). Hillsdale, NJ: Erlbaum.

Marmar, C., Wilner, N., & Horowitz, M. J. (1984). Recurrent patient states in psychotherapy: Segmentation and quantification. In L. Rice & L. Greenberg (Eds.), *Change episodes in psychotherapy* (pp. 194–212). New York: Guilford Press.

Mayman, M. (1968). Early memories and character structure. *Journal of Projective Techniques and Personality Assessment, 32,* 303–316.

Meichenbaum, D., & Gilmore, B. (1984). The nature of unconscious processes: A cognitive behavioral perspective. In K. S. Bower & D. Meichenbaum (Eds.), *The unconscious reconsidered* (pp. 273–298). New York: Wiley.

Modell, A. H. (1975). A narcissistic defense against affects and the illusion of self-sufficiency. *International Journal of Psycho-Analysis, 56,* 275–282.

Muran, J. C., Samstag, L. W., Ventur, E. D., Segal, Z. V., & Winston, A. (2001). A cognitive–interpersonal case study of a self. *Journal of Clinical Psychology, 57,* 307–330.

Neimeyer, R. (1986). *The development of personal construct psychology.* Lincoln: University of Nebraska Press.

Norcross, C. J., & Goldfried, M. R. (Eds.). (1992). *Handbook of psychotherapy integration.* New York: Basic Books.

Perry, J. C., & Cooper, S. H. (1983). An empirical study of defense mechanisms: I. Clinical interview and life vignette ratings. *Archives of General Psychiatry, 46,* 444–452.

Persons, J. B. (1989). *Cognitive therapy in practice: A case formulation approach.* New York: Norton.

Persons, J. B. (1992). A case formulation approach to cognitive–behavior therapy: Application to panic disorder. *Psychiatric Annals, 22,* 470–473.

Piaget, J. (1954). *The construction of reality in the child.* New York: Basic Books. (Original work published 1937)

Rapaport, D. (1967). Cognitive structures. In M. Gill (Ed.), *Collected papers of David Rapaport* (pp. 631–664). New York: Basic Books.

Sampson, H., & Weiss, J. (1986). Testing hypotheses: The approach of the Mount Zion Psychotherapy Research Group. In L. S. Greenberg & W. M. Pinsof (Eds.), *The psychotherapeutic process: A research handbook* (pp. 591–613). New York: Guilford Press.

Sass, L. A. (1992). *Madness and modernism: Insanity in the light of modern art, literature, and thought.* New York: Basic Books.

Schank, R., & Abelson, R. (1977). *Scripts, plans, goals, and understanding.* Hillsdale, NJ: Erlbaum.

Schilder, P. (1950). *The image and appearance of the human body: Studies in the constructive energies of the psyche.* New York: International Universities Press.

Silberschatz, G., Curtis, J. T., & Nathans, S. (1989). Using the patient's plan to assess progress in psychotherapy. *Psychotherapy: Theory, Research, Practice, Training, 26,* 40–46.

Stern, D. N. (1985). *The interpersonal world of the infant*. New York: Basic Books.

Stern, D. N. (1998). The process of therapeutic change involving implicit knowledge: Some implications of developmental observations for adult psychotherapy. *Infant Mental Health Journal, 19*, 300–308.

Stevens, A. (1982). *Archetypes: A natural history of the self*. New York: Morrow.

Stinson, C. H., & Horowitz, M. J. (1993). PSYCLOPS: An exploratory graphical system for clinical research and education. *Psychiatry, 56*, 375–389.

Sullivan, H. S. (1953). *The interpersonal theory of psychiatry*. New York: Norton.

Sundin, E., & Horowitz, M. J. (2002). Horowitz' Impact of Event Scale: Psychometric properties. *British Journal of Psychiatry, 180*, 205–209.

Tomkins, S. (1978). Script theory: Differential magnification of affects. In H. E. Howe (Ed.), *Nebraska Symposium on Motivation* (pp. 201–236). Lincoln: University of Nebraska Press.

Vaillant, G. E. (2002). *Aging well: Surprising guideposts to a happier life from the landmark, Harvard Study of Adult Development*. Boston: Little, Brown.

Vieth, I. (1977). Four thousand years of hysteria. In M. J. Horowitz (Ed.), *Hysterical personality* (pp. 7–93). New York: Aronson.

Wallerstein, R. S. (1986). *Forty-two lives in treatment: A study of psychoanalysis and psychotherapy*. New York: Guilford Press.

Weiss, J. (1993). *How psychotherapy works: Process and technique*. New York: Guilford Press.

Weiss, J., Sampson, H., & the Mount Zion Psychotherapy Research Group. (1986). *The psychoanalytic process: Theory, clinical observation and empirical research*. New York: Guilford Press.

Westen, D. (1990). Toward a revised theory of borderline object relations: Implications of empirical research. *International Journal of Psycho-Analysis, 71*, 661–693.

Wiggins, J. S. (1979). A psychological taxonomy of trait-descriptive terms: The interpersonal domain. *Journal of Personality and Social Psychology, 37*, 395–412.

Wiggins, J. S. (1982). Circumplex models of interpersonal behavior in clinical psychology. In P. C. Kendall & J. N. Butcher (Eds.), *Handbook of research methods in clinical psychology* (pp. 183–221). New York: Wiley.

Young, J. E., & Mattila, D. E. (2002). Schema-focused therapy for depression. In M. A. Reinecke & M. R. Davison (Eds.), *Comparative treatments of depression* (pp. 291–316). New York: Springer.

INDEX

Analysis, 121

Anxiety
    and problematic compromise state,
        35

Approximation of the recurrent self–
    other concepts initially presented
    by Janice (exhibit), 26

Avoidance techniques, 50, 51, 52. *See
    also* Defensive control processes

Awareness, insight, and new decisions
    (figure), 5

Beliefs, dysfunctional, 76

Belief structures, 121

Biological factors, 10, 55
    and interventions, 75

Borderline personality disorder, 6–7, 8

British Object Relations School, 12

Case formulation, 3–4, 13, 66–67. *See*
    Identity and relationships; Phe-
    nomena, observation of; States;
    Topics of concern

Change. *See* Evaluating change

Character, 121

Children
    abuse and trauma of, 64

Cognitive–behavioral therapy (CBT), 55,
    64
    and therapeutic alliance, 91

Configuration, defined, 121

Configuration analysis (CA), 3–5. *See
    also* Connie's case example; Evalu-
    ating change; Identity and rela-
    tionships; Janice's case example;
    Modifying controls; Phenomena,
    observation of; States; Topics of
    concern; Transitions between
    states, modification of; Working
    on views of self and relationships
    defined, 121
    experience at, 35, 119

and obstacles to therapy, 71–72
    review of, 113–118
    steps in, 13
    systematic method of, 13

Configuration of role-relationship models
    (figure), 65

Connie's case example, 113–118
    defensive control processes, 114,
        116, 117
    evaluation of outcome, 117
    phenomena of, 113–114
    relationships in, 114–115, 116, 117
    states of, 144, 115–116
    therapy process, 115–116
    topics of concern, 114, 116, 117

Controls. *See* Modifying controls

Core conflictual relationship theme,
    66–67

Counteracting disavowal, 83–85

Crisis, precipitating, 17–19

Crying state, 41

Death
    as stressor event, 9, 10

Defensive control processes, 11, 24–25,
    47–54, 114, 116, 117. *See also*
    Topics of concern
    case example of, 48–53
    defined, 121

Depression
    case examples of, 18, 36, 72, 114
    and evaluating change, 103
    homesickness topic leading to depres-
        sion (figure), 78
    homesickness topic leading to hope
        (figure), 80
    multiple recurrent states and, 8

Description of states by degree of modula-
    tion (table), 41

Desired states, 26, 35

Disavowal, counteracting, 83–85

Dreaded states, 35, 41, 64

Dyselaboration, 10

Ego
    and states, 7
Emotions. *See also* Identity and relation-
        ships
    and information processing, 8–10
    and self-governance, 8
    and states, 7, 8–10, 33, 56
Evaluating change, 13, 101–111
    case examples of, 101–102, 104–105,
        106–111, 117
    identity and relationships, 103, 117
    modification of self-concepts, 107,
        109, 111
    overview of, 102–103
    phenomena and state of mind,
        102–103
    topics of concern, 103, 117
Evaluation and treatment outcomes. *See*
        Evaluating change; review of con-
        figuration analysis

First approximation of states for Janice
        (exhibit), 24

Histrionic personality disorder, 6–7
Homesickness topic leading to depression
        (figure), 78
Homesickness topic leading to hope
        (figure), 80
Hostility, 33
Hurt and not working state, 26, 41
    case example of, 36, 42, 58, 61, 105
    defined, 63
Hysteria, 6

Identity. *See also* Identity and relation-
        ships
    defined, 121
Identity and relationships, 25–26, 55–68.
        See also Role-relationship models;
        Working on views of self and rela-
        tionships
    case examples of, 60–66, 114–115
    configuration of role-relationship
        models (figure), 65
    core conflictual relationship theme,
        66–67

and evaluating change, 103, 107–
        111, 117
    and formulation of case, 66–67,
        114–115
    and hurt and not working state, 63
    and patterns after therapy, 107
    relationships of Janice's states to
        self-concepts (table), 57
    and role-relationship models, 58–60,
        63–66
    role-relationship models for common
        state transitions (figure), 59, 93
    role relationships for acute self-
        disgust and shame, competitive,
        and acute self-disgust and guilt
        states (figure), 62
    and self-concepts, 57–58
    and transactions, 58
Individual list of states for Janice (ex-
        hibit), 36
Information processing, 8–10
Inhibition, modification of, 80
Initial approximation of topics of concern
        and defense processes for Janice
        (exhibit), 25
Interpersonal psychotherapy (IPT), 55
Interpersonal theories, 11–13

Janice's case example, 13, 17–26, 27–31,
        36–45, 48–53, 60–66, 74–75, 76–
        85, 87–89, 92–97, 101–102, 104–
        105, 106–111
    approximation of the recurrent self–
        other concepts initially presented
        (exhibit), 26
    attitude in therapy, 21
    and early sessions, 27–28
    first approximation of states (ex-
        hibit), 24
    formulation of case, 66–67
    history of, 19–22
    homesickness topic, 20, 77–79,
        81–82
    individual list of states (exhibit), 36
    initial approximation of topics of
        concern and defense processes
        (exhibit), 25
    initial formulation of configuration
        analysis, 22–26

phenomena list for Janice, early
(exhibit), 23, 30
phenomena list for Janice, later
(exhibit), 30
precipitating crisis, 17–19
relationships of states to self-
concepts (table), 57
and role-relationship models, 60–66
self-description, 21–22
and switching maneuvers, 81–83
therapist's initial description of, 22
therapist's states, 75
state transitions (figure), 43

Magical thinking, 121
Mid-course corrections, 3, 13. *See also*
Modifying controls; Transitions
between states, modification of;
Working on views of self and
relationships
Modification of transitions. *See* Transitions between states, modification
of
Modifying controls. *See also* Topics of
concern; Transitions between
states, modification of
case examples of, 76–79, 116
counteracting disavowal, 83–85
effect of therapist on, 79
inhibition, modification of, 80
and switching maneuvers, 81–83

Narcissistic personality disorder, 6–7, 8

Object concepts, 57–58
Observing phenomena. *See* Phenomena,
observation of
Oedipus complex, 11
Overmodulated states, 32, 45, 71
defined, 33, 34, 41, 121

Personality, 121. *See also* Identity and re-
lationships; Personal schemas
Personality trait psychology, 12
Person schemas, 11–13, 122
Phenomena, observation of, 22–23, 29–
30, 113–114. *See also* States;

Transitions between states, modification of
case examples of, 22–23, 29–30,
113–114
and evaluating change, 102–105
and states of mind, 102–103
Phenomena list for Janice, early
(exhibit), 23, 30
Phenomena list for Janice, later
(exhibit), 30
Preconscious processing, 122
Psychodynamic configuration, 122
Psychopathology, 29, 55, 122
Psychotherapy, 4, 122

Regulatory states with general definitions
(exhibit), 34
Relationships. *See* Identity and relationships
Relationships of Janice's states to self-
concepts (table), 57
Representations, 122
Reschematizations, 122
Role-relationship models. *See also* Identity and relationships
for the acute self-disgust and shame,
competitive, and acute self-
disgust and guilt states (figure),
62, 96
case example of, 60–66
for common state transitions
(figure), 59, 93
configurations of, 63–66
configurations of role-relationship
models (figure), 65
defined, 58–60, 122
modification of, 107
as schema, 10, 11
social relationship model, 92–94
and therapeutic alliance, 90–91
and transactions, 58
and working on views of self and
relationships, 89–90

Schemas, 11, 25, 122–123. *See also*
Person schema
Self-analysis, 32

Self-concepts, 11, 56, 57–58
    defined, 123
    modification of, 107, 108, 109, 111
Self-disgust, 41
    and avoidance techniques, 50, 52
    case example of, 41, 42, 44, 52, 61,
        63, 92
    role-relationships for acute self-
        disgust and shame, competitive,
        and acute self-disgust and guilt
        states (figure), 62
Self-organization, 11, 12, 108
    defined, 123
Self-schema, 25, 67, 123. See also Person
        schema
    supraordinate, 11, 123
    unconscious, 11
Self-states, 7
Shame. See Self-disgust
Shimmering state, 10, 32
    defined, 33, 34, 41, 123
Social factors, 10, 55
    and interventions, 75
State analysis, 6–8, 23, 34–36
States, 23–24, 30–31. See also Phenom-
        ena, observation of; State analy-
        sis; Transitions between states,
        modification of
    case examples of, 36–44, 114,
        115–116
    compromise, 35
    cycles of, 44–45, 121
    defined, 6, 31–32, 123
    description of by degree of modula-
        tion (table), 41
    desired, 26, 35
    dreaded, 35, 41, 64
    dynamics of, 45
    and emotionality, 7, 8–10, 33
    and evaluating change, 103,
        103–105
    and expressions of emotions, 7
    hurt and not working, 26, 41, 63
    labels of, 32, 35
    motivational categories of, 35
    multiple, 8
    overmodulated, 33, 34, 41, 45, 122
    and phenomena, 102–103
    problematic compromise, 35
    regulatory with general definitions
        (exhibit), 34

shimmering, 10, 32, 33, 34, 41, 123
tra-la-la, 26, 41
transitions between, 42–44
undermodulated, 30, 33, 34, 41, 123
well-modulated, 32, 33, 34, 41, 73,
    123–124
States, controls, and persons schemas in
    relation to awareness, insight,
    and decision making (table), 6
Step 1 in configuration analysis. See
    Phenomena, observation of
Step 2 in configuration analysis. See
    States
Step 3 in configuration analysis. See
    Topics of concern
Step 4 in configuration analysis. See
    Identity and relationships
Step 5 in configuration analysis. See
    Transitions between states,
    modification of
Step 6 in configuration analysis. See
    Modifying controls
Step 7 in configuration analysis. See
    Working on views of self and
    relationships
Step 8 in configuration analysis. See
    Evaluating change
Switching maneuvers, 81–83

Therapeutic alliance, 89, 90–91. See also
    Therapists
    case example of, 92, 111
    defined, 123
    difficulties in establishing, 95
    and learning new attitudes, 95–96
Therapists, 119. See also Therapeutic
        alliance
    effect on controls, 79
    effect on transitions between states,
        74–75
    states of, 75
    and therapeutic alliance with
        patient, 89, 90–91, 111
Topics of concern, 24–25, 47–54, 114,
        116, 117. See also Modifying
        controls
    case examples of, 48–53, 114
    and dysfunctional beliefs, 47
    and evaluating change, 103,
        105–107

and patient discrepancies, 48

Tra-la-la state, 26, 41
    case example of, 36, 42, 44, 58, 60,
        71, 74, 92, 94, 104, 110

Transactions, 58
    defined, 123

Transference, 94–95, 123

Transitions between states, modification
    of, 71–86. *See also* Phenomena,
    observation of; States
    case examples of, 74, 115–116
    effect of therapist on, 74–75
    reviewing phenomena changes, 72
    tracking phenomena, 73–74

Transitions between states of Janice (fig-
    ure), 43

Triad of awareness, insight, and new deci-
    sions (figure), 5

Undermodulated states, 30, 41
    defined, 33, 34, 123

Videotapes, used in configurations, 12
    case example of, 75

Well-modulated states, 32, 73
    defined, 33, 34, 41, 123–124

Working model, 124

Working on views of self and relation-
    ships, 87–98. *See also* Identity
    and relationships
    case examples of, 91–97, 116
    learning new attitudes, 95–96
    role-relationship for the acute self-
        disgust and shame, competitive,
        and acute self-disgust and guilt
        states (figure), 62
    and role-relationship models, 89–90
    role-relationship models for common
        state transitions (figure), 59, 93
    social relationship model, 92–94
    therapeutic alliance, 89, 90–91
    and transferences, 94–95

ABOUT THE AUTHOR

Mardi Horowitz, MD, is professor of psychiatry at the University of California, San Francisco, where he has initiated and directed clinical research programs, including the Psychotherapy Evaluation and Study Center, the Center for the Study of Neuroses, the Program on Conscious and Unconscious Mental Processes, and the Center on Stress and Personality. His work with these projects, especially his work contributing to the diagnosis and treatment of posttraumatic stress disorder, culminated in receiving the Lifetime Achievement Award from the International Society for Traumatic Stress Studies. He has received numerous other awards throughout his career, including the Foundations Fund Prize for Psychiatric Research and the Hibbs Award, both from the American Psychiatric Association, as well as the Royer Award from the University of California Regents.

His research on a cognitive–psychodynamic theory and on diagnosis, formulation, and brief therapy was summarized in several successful books, including *Stress Response Syndromes*, *Treatment of Stress Response Syndromes*, and *Formulation as a Basis for Psychotherapy Treatment*. His most recent work has focused on integrating treatments and, to that end, he has collaborated on two textbooks aimed at deepening cognitive science to include verifiable psychodynamic processes: *Introduction to Psychodynamics: A New Synthesis* and *Cognitive Psychodynamics: From Conflict to Character*.